Essays on Her Works

WRITERS SERIES 1

SERIES EDITORS:
ANTONIO D'ALFONSO AND JOSEPH PIVATO

Canada

Guernica Editions Inc. acknowledges the support of
The Canada Council for the Arts.
Guernica Editions Inc. acknowledges the support of
the Ontario Arts Council.
Guernica Editions Inc. acknowledges the financial support of the
Government of Canada through the Book Publishing Industry
Development Program (BPIDP).

SHARON POLLOCK

Essays on Her Works

Edited by Anne F. Nothof

GUERNICA
TORONTO • BUFFALO • LANCASTER (U.K.)
2000

Copyright © 2000, by Anne F. Nothof and Guernica Editions Inc.
All rights reserved. The use of any part of this publication, reproduced,
transmitted in any form or by any means, electronic, mechanical,
photocopying, recording or otherwise stored in a retrieval system, without
the prior consent of the publisher is an infringement of the copyright law.

Anne F. Nothof, Editor.
Guernica Editions Inc.
P.O. Box 117, Station P, Toronto (ON), Canada M5S 2S6
2250 Military Road, Tonawanda, N.Y. 14150-6000 U.S.A.
Gazelle, Falcon House, Queen Square, Lancaster LA1 1RN U.K.

Typesetting by Selina.
Printed in Canada.

Legal Deposit – Second Quarter
National Library of Canada
Library of Congress Catalog Card Number: 00-101686

Canadian Cataloguing in Publication Data
Main entry under title:
Sharon Pollock : essays on her works
(Writers series ; 1)
Includes bibliographical references.
ISBN 1-55071-108-3
1. Pollock, Sharon – Criticism and interpretation.
I. Nothof, Anne. II. Series: Writers series (Toronto, Ont.) ; 1.
PS8581.034Z87 2000 C812'.54 C00-900962-0
PR9199.3.P57Z87 2000

Contents

Acknowledgements	6
Introduction: Illuminating the Facets by Anne F. Nothof	7
Sharon Pollock: Committed Playwright by Malcolm Page	12
Sharon Pollock's Plays: A Review Article by Robert C. Nunn	26
Sharon Pollock's Women: A Study in Dramatic Process by Diane Bessai	44
Feminism and Metadrama: Role Playing in *Blood Relations* by Susan Stratton	68
Crossing Borders: Sharon Pollock's Revisitation of Canadian Frontiers by Anne F. Nothof	81
Broken Toys: The Destruction of the National Hero in the Early History Plays of Sharon Pollock by Heidi J. Holder	100
Women and Madness: Sharon Pollock's Plays of the Early 1990s by Craig Stewart Walker	128
"Lookin' to a better world for our children": The Concept of Inheritance in Pollock's *Fair Liberty's Call* by Kathy K. Y. Chung	151
Sharon Pollock Interview with Sharon Pollock by Anne F. Nothof	167
Biography of Sharon Pollock	180
Bibliography	183
Contributors	191

Acknowledgements

Malcolm Page. "Sharon Pollock: Committed Playwright." *Canadian Drama*, 5.2 (Fall 1979): 104-111. Reproduced with the permission of the author.

Robert Nunn. "Sharon Pollock's Plays: A Review Article." *Theatre History in Canada*, 5.1 (Spring 1984): 72-83. Reproduced with the permission of the author.

Diane Bessai. "Sharon Pollock's Women: A Study in Dramatic Process." *A Mazing Space: Writing Canadian Women Writing*, eds. Shirley Neuman and Smaro Kamboureli. Edmonton: Longspoon/NeWest Press, 1986: 126-136. Reproduced with the permission of the author and the editors of NeWest Press.

Susan Stratton. "Feminism and Metadrama: Role Playing in *Blood Relations*. Originally published under Susan Stone-Blackburn in *Canadian Drama*, 15.2 (1989): 169-178. Reproduced with the permission of the author.

Anne F. Nothof. "Crossing Borders: Sharon Pollock's Revisitation of Canadian Frontiers." *Modern Drama*, 38 (Winter 1995): 475-487. Reproduced with the permission of the author.

Heidi Holder. "Broken Toys: The Destruction of the National Hero in the Early History Plays of Sharon Pollock." *Essays in Theatre*, 14.2 (1996): 131-45. Reproduced with the permission of the author and the editors of *Essays in Theatre*.

Craig Stewart Walker. "Women and Madness: Sharon Pollock's Plays of the Early 1990s." Based on material taken from the forthcoming book *Desperate Wilderness: Canadian Dramatic Imagination and Western Tradition*. Toronto: McGill-Queen's Press, 1999. Published with the permission of the author and McGill-Queen's Press.

Introduction

Illuminating the Facets

Anne F. Nothof

During her more than thirty years as a playwright, actor, director, dramaturge, teacher, and theatre administrator, Sharon Pollock has been committed to "getting it straight" – probing preconceptions and assumptions, both political and personal. But she also acknowledges that the means of "getting it straight" are necessarily indirect and partial, the "truths" various and fragmented. Pollock uses the image of a diamond to demonstrate the various possibilities inherent in any story, and the many points of view from which it may be told:

> It's as if truthfulness when you're writing about life is a big multi-faceted diamond. I am standing in one place, and I am the result of a certain time and place and experience, and I have a flashlight. If I never try to expand those boundaries I can only hold my flashlight one way, shine it on one part of the diamond. By being aware of how I do see through certain eyes and in a certain way, I get to expand, I get to be able to move the light.
>
> But I can't go all the way around that diamond. So when I tell the story of Walsh or Sitting Bull, I may be shining my flashlight on a certain portion of that diamond. The First Nation person who is beside me is in a different place, but the same position I am. I suppose when you have many writers attacking the same story, you get the entire diamond lit up.

> I think that I can write a story so long as I find a way within the structure of the story to acknowledge my angle of observation. I'm the result of my middle-class, white upbringing in a conservative part of the country, in a racist country, in a colonized country, next to the largest, most powerful country in the world. I am aware of that and I try to educate myself and sensitize myself to how that has formed me, so that I can understand and overcome the limitations that it's put on me – but to believe that I could ever manage to get rid of all that is a great lie (*Airborne* 100-101).

Pollock may fracture point of view through a multiple perspective on historical events, as she does in *Fair Liberty's Call*, or through the fragmented unfocused monologue of a woman who sees the world from beneath the grandstand of the Calgary Stampede in *Getting it Straight*. In *The Making of Warriors*, a radio play commissioned by the CBC to coincide with the Second International Women Playwrights Conference in Toronto in May 1991, Pollock shines her flashlight on the lives of two women social activists from two different centuries to show the interaction of past and present, and the interplay of historical "fact" and fictionalized "event" – the multiple ironies inherent in history.

Pollock's fascination with history is evident in most of her plays – from *Walsh* (1973) to the one that she began writing in 1999, *End Dream*, which is based on the "true" story of a young Scottish nanny who was murdered in Vancouver in the 1920s, and the consequent persecution of a Chinese servant. She investigates the variant tellings of each story, and scrutinizes the inherent ideologies – the issues of power and control. In other words, she gives each character a different point of view on events. Particularly for the women in her plays, this "telling" is a strategy of empowerment, "the ability to take one's place in whatever discourse is essential to action and the right to have one's part matter" (Heilbrun 3). On the other hand, Pollock distrusts power, and a major theme in her plays in accountability.

In *Doc* (1984) and in *Moving Pictures* (1999), the women's stories are refracted through multiple personas enacting different stages of their lives. The past is enacted in the present: one facet of character illuminates another. In *Doc*, an adolescent "Katie" is observed from the perspective of an adult "Catherine." In *Moving Pictures*, the silent film actress and producer, Nell Shipman, ironically observes her younger ambitious selves as a precocious and talented teenage actor and as an independent producer of films, and wonders whether her work and life have any significance or consequence. The definition of "moving pictures" which is repeated like a choric refrain in the play could serve as a comment on the ephemeral nature of any theatrical event, but also its potential to evoke a living image. As defined by Thomas Edison, film is "the illusion of continuous movement through persistence of vision." This "persistence of vision" is both Nell's strength and her downfall. She cannot compromise it, and so compromises both her personal and her professional life. As the play illustrates, film can be burned if it is placed too close to the projector. *Moving Pictures* is a portrait of the artist as older woman. Pollock poses questions that continue to preoccupy her: Can you be an artist if your work can't find an audience? What motivates an artist when there is no recognition? Why make personal sacrifices for a vision? Was it worth it? What is "it"? Pollock admits to not being sure she'll ever understand why she's made the sacrifices she has, and admits it is something that preoccupies her but also motivates her: "It is the parts of myself and the world that I don't like that I find the most interesting to write about" (quoted in MacMillan). As in many of her plays, the possibility of "choice" and the consequences of choice are scrutinized.

For Pollock, writing plays is only one facet of her commitment to theatre as a means of illuminating the dark corners of apathy and ignorance. She has acted, in her own plays, as well as in others, taught playwriting at the University of Alberta, led the playwrights' colony at the Banff Centre, and has been artistic director of Theatre Calgary (1984) and Theatre New Brunswick (1988-90). In 1992, she started her own theatre in Calgary, the Garry, as a community theatre with integral connections to the life of the city. Under the management of her son, Kirk Campbell, the Garry produced a wide range of works: *Macbeth, Billy Bishop Goes to War, The Tomorrow Box, Come Back to the Five and Dime, Jimmy Dean, Death of a Salesman, Nurse Jane Goes to Hawaii, Heading Out*, and her own new plays *A Death in the Family* and *Saucy Jack*. Without government subsidies, however, the Garry was not financially viable and it closed in 1997. She is now closely involved with Theatre Junction in Calgary, where *Moving Pictures* premiered in 1999 and *End Dream* in 2000. In 1999, she also directed a production of Pinter's *Betrayal* for Theatre Junction.

As Robert Nunn presaged in his review article on Pollock, written fifteen years ago, "with her long-haul commitment to the discipline, with her experimentation, and expansion of the boundaries of her dramatic universe," Sharon Pollock may be now regarded as "Canada's answer to Ibsen." The essays in this monograph track her career through the early "history plays" to the more recent "feminist plays," although Pollock's works, as does Pollock herself, defy categories. These essays only begin to examine the richness of her work in terms of its text and its theatricality. For Pollock, a script is a blueprint for production and, with each performance, new facets are illuminated.

WORKS CITED

Heilbrun, Carolyn. *Writing a Woman's Life*. New York: Ballantine, 1988.

Jansen, Ann, ed. Introduction to "The Making of Warriors," *Airborne: Radio Plays by Women*. Winnipeg: Blizzard, 1991.

MacMillan, Shannon. "Backpage," *Where*, March 1999.

Sheppy, Nikki. "Theatre Preview," *FFWD* 4.11.

Sharon Pollock: Committed Playwright

Malcolm Page

Sharon Pollock may be an underestimated writer because, of her numerous works, only *Walsh* (Talonbooks) and *The Komagata Maru Incident* (Playwrights Co-op) are readily available – for the fact (sometimes the accident) of publication remains important in establishing the stature of a playwright. Further, Pollock identifies with alternative rather than mainstream theatre, telling an interviewer: "I don't feel a part of the theatre community. I'm glad I'm not – they have tunnel vision. I want community link-ups, to the Sikh community, for example . . . I think I'm writing for people who never go to the theatre . . . I see what other people see but don't recognise, like the poor. That's my job as an artist" (Pollock, "Interview" 1977).

Her first full-length play was *A Compulsory Option*, given a few performances in August 1972 at Vancouver Art Gallery by the New Play Centre (from whom the script is available). Three young male teachers are assigned to share a house, apparently somewhere in rural British Columbia. One is paranoid: he was once a student activist, who protested the cafeteria blancmange, but it rained during his protest, and no one came. Now the mailman constantly brings letters to his address for people he doesn't know, and drivers try to run over his toes. The second starts out as baffled straightman to his eccentricities, then gradually comes to share his paranoia. And the third is homosexual (he teaches P.E.) and their victim, accidentally wounded when tied to a chair at the end of Act 1. *A Compulsory Option* features a lot of comic visual business with hiding in wardrobes, going in and out through windows, and attempting to assemble rifles from a mass of hinges and bits of coffee percolators. Pleasingly absurdist, I find a good deal of fun in *A Compulsory Option*, but all Pollock's plays since have been more political and "relevant."

Walsh followed, written first for radio, then being staged at Calgary in November 1973 and at the Stratford Festival the next year, in a revised text (Talonbooks published both versions). *Walsh* is the first of Pollock's plays drawn from history; she says, "I read history because I love history. I began with an interest in *Walsh* as a character, as a rebel. Then I discovered John A. MacDonald had written, 'If words will not prevail with the Sioux, hunger will.' I was angry at my own ignorance, and that the historians hadn't told me. I didn't know about the *Komagata Maru* either, and something like it could happen now and I might not know about it" (Pollock, "Lecture" 1976).

Pollock in *Walsh* wants both to challenge the idea, still prevalent among students, that Canada's history is a dull one, of laws, reports, constitutions and boring and indistinguishable politicians, and to direct attention to neglected aspects of that history. (Many other contemporaries have shared this concern, among them Michael Cook in *Colour the Flesh the Colour of Dust*, Herschel Hardin in *The Great Wave of Civilization*, Rick Salutin and Passe Muraille in *1837*, Arthur Murphy in *The First Falls on Monday*, and Ann Henry in *Lulu Street*). In *Walsh* Pollock looks at the greatest of Canadian myths, the Mounties, those glamorous red-coated heroes. She is disturbed most specifically by the treatment of Indians, which is part of her message for the present. Harold Baldridge, director of the Calgary production, commented: "I believe we have made our audience think about our responsibility to and our responsibility for the modern-day problems of the Plains and Woods Indians. I think that not one of us will ever be able to regard a drunken Indian on the street corner in quite the same way" (*CTR* 120).

Pollock has much information to give, so frequently depends on messengers for accounts of Custer's last stand, the flight of Chief Joseph and the Nez Perce, the death of Crazy Horse, the entry of Chief Sitting Bull and his Sioux into Canada, the decline of the buffalo herds, and finally, the killing of Sitting Bull. She paints a broad panorama of the Prairies in the 1870s, in short scenes on a multiple set, for the police fort, Walsh's office, a store room, Indian tents and the open prairie. Representatives of the various groups appear: Mrs. Anderson, the pioneer settler; Crow Eagle and White Dog, the Canadian Indians; Louis, the Métis; Clarence, the new Mountie recruit. The first version of the play has speeches through the loudspeaker preceding each of the twelve scenes, "taken," notes Pollock, "from documents of the day." These are not so much Pollock determinedly educating her audiences, as adequately informing them. The later version, however, discards this awkward device. (It also adds Walsh's wife and a Prologue, set much later, in the Klondike in 1898, where we learn how corrupt Walsh had become, and of course wonder why he had changed.)

Pollock's task as dramatist is to cover Sitting Bull's four years in Canada, including the Indians' way of life, the central situation of the conflict between Sitting Bull and Walsh, and the conflicts within Walsh. Further, much of the real power, of decision-making, is held in Ottawa,

London, and Washington, while settlers, traders, and other Indian tribes have also to be taken into account. Indian instinctive perception of the world contrasts with white scientific knowledge, when Sitting Bull instructs his son Crowfoot, watched by Clarence (59-61). Louis sums this up: "Take all da books, da news dat da white man prints, take all dat bible book, take all dose things you learn from – lay dem on da prairie – and da sun . . . da rain . . . da snow . . . pouf! You wanna learn, you study inside here *[taps head]* . . . and here *[taps chest]* . . . and how it is wit' you and me *[indicates]* . . . and how it is wit' you and all *[indicates surroundings]*. Travel 'round da Medicine Wheel. Den you know somethin'" (27-28). At the end the Mounties play at being Indians and ambush a train, behaving like Indians in movies: the Indians we have seen in the play have done nothing like this.

Sitting Bull remains a remote figure. Urjo Kareda wrote of the first version: "The characterization of Sitting Bull himself is a catastrophe, a portrait of the noble savage so noble and pious and dignified that he has no reality" (*Toronto Star*). Kareda's view ignores both Sitting Bull as mystic and shaman, and as the victim of circumstances over which he has no control. Walsh is an appealing figure for much of the play: full of humanitarian feelings, while loyal and dutiful (and a workaholic willing to remain apart from the wife he loves). Clarence is third in importance, full at first of boyish relish for the fighting of which he knows little: "An Indjun War! . . . I could get to kill the man who killed Custer" (22). He changes, giving his coat to a freezing Indian child (56), then accepting "our Indians" (73) and protesting, "You don't let people starve! You can't do things like that" (75), finally sharing a pipe with Sitting Bull (94), so that Walsh concludes of him, "That young man should never make the Force his life"

(107). Clarence's moral ascent parallels Walsh's decline. *Walsh* is one of the finest Canadian historical plays – and the dilemma of the liberal torn between his duty and his principles can be found as easily in the present.

The next play, *And Out Goes You*, is more overtly political. Performed on the mainstage at Vancouver Playhouse in March 1975, this depicts a family about to be evicted from their East Vancouver home by government and business interests, as theirs is the last property delaying some massive re-development. The family consists of the father, George, a veteran of Dunkirk, two sons, a 1967-vintage hippie with a drum and a former mailman whose worldly knowledge is derived solely from mail he never delivered, and a daughter, the responsible breadwinner, whose part is thin and under-written. As no one is able to sign the documents for expropriation, the young bureaucrat suggests forgery. Next the Premier (played by Owen Foran, trying hard to look like the then-Premier, Dave Barrett) and the Chairman (Michael Ball, probably intended to resemble Bill Bennett) enter and praise highrise developments. They distribute buttons with the ambiguous slogan "Know Your Place" – where the people will be re-located in the tower blocks, but also that the masses should not question their niche in society. Act 2 features the revival of the grandmother, Goose, who has been in a coma for forty years as a result of injury in the Dominion Day riot in Regina in 1935, who is restored by being dropped downstairs. She tries to rally the family and the bureaucrat to go out and lead a mass protest against the eviction and against the whole political machine. They kidnap the Premier and the Chairman and enact a little "guerilla theatre" for them, then Goose is shot and reverts to paralysis.

Thus *And Out Goes You* has disparate elements: a plausible 1975 situation, with at least two near-real characters, and others mentioned, like Social Credit personality, Phil Gaglardi; comic-absurd characters in inconsequential comedy; and the symbolic Goose. Christopher Newton, the director, recognised the problem in his programme note: "This is not a naturalistic comedy, neither is it derived from the theatre of the absurd. It has its feet firmly on the ground, but at the same time the fantasies of the inhabitants of the house and the fear of the politicians are given theatrical form." *And Out Goes You* can easily be seen as a play like Brendan Behan's *The Hostage*, a real and serious situation glanced at amidst songs and a crowd of bizarre characters in a slum house. Or it might present clearly the message articulated by Newton: "The point is that regardless of who sits in power, significant change only occurs when all individuals of a society recognize and exercise their responsibilities for change" (Allen, "Laughs Aimed" 35). Pollock expressed it as, "When we put someone else at the head of the pyramid, then we call it change. The tip of a pyramid is its smallest part. Obviously, real change only occurs when the broad base is altered. The collection of individuals in a society is that base. They must change if anything meaningful is to happen" (Allen, "Laughs Aimed" 35).

I found that *And Out Goes You* failed in performance. There had, perhaps, been too many re-writes, too much input from the Tamahnous group and the New Play Centre during workshops and from director and actors in rehearsal. Perhaps the spirit of the unemployed in Regina in 1935, vital though it was for Pollock, was never clearly put into the text. Perhaps the sense of politics was insufficiently exact and the sense of ordinary working-class people too woolly and sentimental. Perhaps the play was distorted by Playhouse publicity which suggested audiences were to see a satire on the N.D.P. government. Or perhaps the tone was too unconventional to be captured by any group in a standard rehearsal-period.

Pollock has remained close to the material, drawing on it for the one-act *Mail vs. Female* (Lunchbox Theatre, Calgary, March 1979). She told me: "I know I am going to adapt and use other things in it. Georgie and Goose are two characters I'm very fond of and I intend to rework the material yet again in a bigger form than the one-act" (Pollock, "Letter to Page").

Pollock returned to history, and ventured further from the well-made form, with *The Komagata Maru Incident*. This 75-minute piece was staged by the Playhouse at Vancouver East Cultural Centre in January 1976 and revived at the Citadel, Edmonton, a year later. *The Komagata Maru* brought 376 East Indians to Vancouver in May 1914, and they were not allowed to land. The night the ship docked Sir Richard McBride, the B.C. Premier, stated: "To admit Orientals in large numbers would mean in the end the extinction of the white people, and we always have in mind the necessity of keeping this a white man's country" (Ferguson 10). The ship remained in the harbour for two months, during which racist feelings grew and various legal proceedings occurred, and the vessel eventually was forced to leave. Pollock, however, is less concerned with expounding facts than she had been in *Walsh*: "Theatre should hit people emotionally, in my opinion, and that is my intention with this play. That is why I'm trying to avoid the documentary flavour because, to learn and understand, the people of the situation must be put across" (Allen, "Play Reveals" 31). She explains in a Note with the text that the drama "is a theatrical impression of an historical event seen through the optique of the stage and the mind of the playwright . . . To encompass these facts, time and place are often compressed, and certain dramatic licence is employed" (v). Further, the message to the present is most important for her, as she wrote in the programme: "To know where we are going, we must know where we have been and what we have come from. Our attitudes towards the non-white peoples of the world and of Canada is one that suffers from the residual effects of centuries of oppressive policies which were given moral and ethical credence by the fable of racial superiority . . . The attitudes expressed by the general populace of that time, and paraphrased throughout the play, are still around today and, until we face this fact, we can never change it." Not only has the Vancouver area experienced tensions towards the East Indians in the 1970s; as I write, Canada is considering how many Asian refugee "boat people" to admit.

Pollock's treatment of the "incident" centres on William Hopkinson, who led a double life as an Immigration Department official and undercover spy, disguised as an East Indian, trying to detect sedition. He is murdered by a Sikh in the Court House at the end of the drama. Half East Indian himself, he repudiated that part of his past and tried to act as more Canadian than the Canadians. Walsh's conflict between duty and humanity recurs in Hopkinson, but this time the conflict is uneven.

Pollock's stagecraft is more sophisticated here than in *Walsh*. No longer is there a sense that the work should really have been a film (Pollock has said that she would have preferred her Sioux on horseback). Nor does she need representatives of each of the groups involved: lawyers and Premiers are not shown and the cast is only six. The incident, with its ramifications and continuing implications, is approached obliquely. A master of ceremonies, a greasy barker and magician, with gloves, hat and cane, plays various parts, gives explanations, manipulates his characters and suggests a carnival mood. Known as T.S., he has been taken as The System, though Pollock explains that she wanted to avoid writing "No.1" or "A," and the initials of T.S. Eaton had somehow stuck in her mind (Dunn 5). He suggests Joel Grey in *Cabaret* and provides a frame recalling *O What a Lovely War!* Short and overlapping turns hurry through the story of Hopkinson, the events on board the Komagata Maru, and life in a seedy brothel frequented by Hopkinson. Through it all one woman, with an unseen child, stands, dignified though pathetic, in a kind of cage at the back of the stage, representing all the unfortunate East Indians. The published text does not attempt to describe the fine set Jack Simons provided in Vancouver, apparently made of rotting material starting to fall apart. While *The Komagata Maru Incident* was theatrically effective in Vancouver, its message was direct but not obtrusive. Pollock shows the part played in racism by fear and ignorance, and shows equally officialdom, with its unscrupulous readiness to bend regulations.

In *Komagata Maru* Pollock provided three parts for women in describing an "incident" which was almost all male. The feminist commitment was clearer in *My Name Is Lisbeth*, staged, with Pollock herself in the title-role, in a student production at Douglas College, Surrey, B.C., at the end of March, 1976. The work is being revised for production by Theatre New Brunswick in the 1979-80 season, re-titled *Blood Relations*[1];I write of the original version.

The subject is Lizzie Borden, the celebrated Massachusetts murderess of 1892, who, as Pollock pointed out in an otherwise uninformative programme note, legally changed her name from Lizzie, as christened, to Lisbeth soon after the murders. Again, Pollock researched thoroughly: "I've read pretty well everything written about Lizzie Borden, and many related books and articles on murders, women, and the age she lived in" (Anon, "Ax Murder"). Pollock's intention was predictable, to show that Lizzie could not fulfil the daughterly role laid down for her: "What happened to her is an exaggerated example of what still happens today" (Anon., "Ax Murder").

The play is in about a dozen episodes, mostly duologues, interspersed with a few monologues: a couple of characters introduce themselves, and Lizzie has several semi-poetic soliloquies. The first act presents scenes from the day before the murders; the second, the day of the murders. The household has six members. Lizzie proclaims that she hates her fat vacuous stepmother, for no apparent reason but that she is a stepmother; three times a reference to her "mother" is savagely corrected by Lizzie to "stepmother." Her father is sixty-four, kindly but rigid in his thinking about women and ownership. Emma, her elder sister, is potentially the most interesting character, as she had the same experiences, but didn't turn murderous. She is pretty, vacillating, apparently encouraging Lizzie to conform. The maid is young, lively, irreverent, and encouraged in her irreverence by Lizzie. Uncle Harry, staying in the house, is distinguished mainly by his lecherous dives at the poor maid (one of the few laughs comes when he is caught in mid-dive). From the outside world comes Dr. Patrick, a married man with whom Lizzie chats shamelessly in public.

Lizzie is shown in the first act as a rebellious misfit. She enters as Uncle Harry leaves on the opposite side, and her opening line, directed at him, is "Silly bugger." Soon after she is encouraging Dr. Patrick to run away with her to Boston, "for a start." We wonder, however, why this strong woman of thirty-four has not found ways of breaking out of the prison long before. The day brings new irritations for Lizzie: her father is inviting round a widower with three sons who might want to marry Lizzie, which prompts the outburst of crockery-throwing; he is working with Uncle Harry at transferring ownership of the farm to his wife, instead of allowing Lizzie and Emma to inherit on his death; finally – mysteriously angered by some break-in – he kills Lizzie's much-loved pigeons with an axe, which ends the first act.

The second act begins with sister Emma leaving for a few days' visit. Lizzie refuses to go with her, yet all the same feels abandoned. Dialogues with father, uncle, mother, maid and Dr. Patrick follow. While the intent seems to be to show a new, determined Lizzie, the conversations add little to what we already know. Then she follows stepmother upstairs, axe behind her back, kills her offstage, changes her clothes helped by the maid, and is disturbed by her father's return before she has had time to establish her alibi. So she lures him to sleep on the sofa so that he will not find out her crime and stop loving her, then kills him, with a strobe light effect to distance the violence.

Pollock, in focusing on episodes, some crucial and others trivial or typical, from the day and a half preceding the murders, and in concluding with the second murder, clearly had a sense of the relentless advance of time toward an end all know is coming. But the advance of time was muffled; a first act reference to "come in, it's nearly lunch-time" lost its effect when much later a line revealed that it was still before lunch. A tighter play, though perhaps one more melodramatic than Pollock would wish to write, would have involved the audience more fully and precisely in the steady advance of time towards the inevitable outcome.

My Name Is Lisbeth comes out as a thin and tentative look at Victorian middle-class family life, by *The Heiress* out of *The Barretts of Wimpole Street*. Detail is lacking: do these people go to church? of what denomination? what is the appeal of a house on the hill, which Lizzie would like to go to, compared with their home? how affluent are they? (a late reference to father being worth half a million dollars suggests far more wealth than I had supposed). Language and manners could be far more precise: nothing is done with the maid twice sitting in the living-room in the presence of her employers, and father says "goddam" in the presence of his wife (reading of Emily Dickinson or watching *Upstairs, Downstairs* teaches alertness to such nuances!).

No clear view of Lizzie, nor reason for writing, comes through. Lizzie Borden's is the best-known American murder (the British have Jack the Ripper), yet Pollock doesn't ask why this is one of the most widely-shared myths (Reaney embroidered the Canadian myth of the Donnellys for nine hours). She seems uninterested in a psychological study (attempted in a 1975 American television play about the infamous Lizzie), though the monologues occasionally suggest moments of insanity. Neither does she write of the problems of the actual case, for the real-life Lizzie was acquitted. Pollock's excited curiosity about the past, evident in the earlier plays, is almost absent this time. While I had anticipated that the central point was to be the oppression of women in Victorian society, with a moral for the present, this is not emphasized.

Pollock has been prolific since *Lisbeth*. *One Tiger to a Hill*, suggested by the hostage-taking and death of Mary

Steinhauser at B.C. Penitentiary in New Westminster in 1975, has been completed for the Citadel, Edmonton. She has written two children's plays for Alberta Theatre Projects and extensively for CBC radio.

Pollock's evolution and purposes are defined as a growing feminism, from the all-male *Compulsory Option* to *My Name Is Lisbeth*, by Margo Dunn in her article in *Makara*. Pollock herself in the article defines a broader concern: "One of the dangers of writing political plays is that I will stop here, that I won't do anything more about class oppression" (5). Though I have drawn most attention to Pollock's ideas and messages, equally striking is her stagecraft, her restless determination to avoid obvious approaches and search for angles which are effective and unusual. What she needs, perhaps, is close and continuing association with a sympathetic company, of the kind enjoyed in Britain by David Edgar with the General Will and John McGrath with the 7:84 Company.[2]

NOTES

1   Pollock tells me that the revised version begins long after the murders, when Lizzie Borden was living in Boston and ending a relationship with an actress. The new text has more characters, includes court-room scenes and develops the picture of Lizzie's later life.

2   A note, twenty years later: I should record first that Pollock returned to *Walsh* in 1983, adding a scene with the American General Terry. This version is to be found in *Modern Canadian Plays*, 1, ed. Jerry Wasserman (Talonbooks, 1993). Her rewriting of the Lizzie Borden story as *Blood Relations* greatly improves on *My Name Is Lisbeth*, which I saw and describe. Looking back at this essay, I find that I seized on the feminism of *My Name Is Lisbeth* and the political position in *Walsh*, *And Out Goes You*, and *Komagata Maru* to fit Pollock into the "committed" fashion of the 1960s, one derived from Sartre's late 1940s view of the need for literature to be *engagé*. Soon

after the term "commitment" came to be used so loosely as to be unhelpful, while Pollock's plays of the 1980s and 90s have gone in more varied directions than I might have predicted. I commented on her plays of 1972-76: there is now a career of nearly thirty years to be assessed.

A note, April 2000: I should note that Pollock returned to *Walsh* in 1983 to add a scene with the American, General Terry. This version is to be found in *Modern Canadian Plays,* Vol. 1, ed. Jerry Wasserman (Talon, 1993). Her rewriting of the Lizzie Borden story as *Blood Relations* greatly improves the *My Name Is Lisbeth,* which I saw and describe. Looking back at this essay, I realise that I seized on the feminism of *My Name Is Leisbeth* and the overt political positions seen in *Walsh, And Out Goes You* and *Komagata Maru to* fit Pollock into the "committed" ideal of the 1960s, one derived from Sartre's late 1940s view of literature's need to be *engagé.* Soon after the term "commitment" came to be used so loosely as to be unhelpful, while Pollock's work of the 1980s and 90s has gone in various directions which could not be predicted. I wrote of her plays of 1972-76: there is now a career of nearly thirty years to be assessed.

Works Cited

Allen, Bob. "Laughs Aimed at Politicians in a New Play." *Province* 21 March 1975: 35.

Allen, Bob. "Play Reveals Shame of Komagata Maru." *Province* 16 January 1976: 31.

Anon. "Ax Murder Theme for College Play." *Pinion.* Douglas College, 26 January 1976.

Baldridge, Harold. *Canadian Theatre Review,* 3 (1974).

Dunn, Margo. "Sharon Pollock: In the Centre Ring." *Makara,* 1.5 (August-September 1976): 2-6.

Ferguson, Ted. *A White Man's Country.* Toronto: Doubleday, 1975.

Kareda, Urjo. *Toronto Star* 13 November 1973.

Pollock, Sharon. *Interview on Co-op Radio.* Vancouver, BC, 13 February 1977.

Pollock, Sharon. *Lecture at Simon Fraser University.* Burnaby, BC, 25 March 1976.

Pollock, Sharon. "Letter to Malcolm Page." 26 February 1979.

Sharon Pollock's Plays

A Review Article

Robert C. Nunn

Since Malcolm Page's article on Sharon Pollock appeared in *Canadian Drama* in 1979, you might say that she has arrived: there has been recognition in the sincerest form, namely productions of new plays on stages across Canada, there has been the publication of *Blood Relations and Other Plays* and its receipt of the Governor General's Literary Award in 1981, there have been awards in the fields of both radio and television drama. It is time for another critical survey of her work.

It must be noted at the outset that we are dealing with only a small part of her work, primarily the published playscripts.[1] The problem of availability noted by Malcolm Page is compounded by the fact that all through her career Sharon Pollock has been writing not only for the stage but for radio and television: her work in both of these media is difficult to get at, yet would have to be considered in any full account. Indeed this aspect of Sharon Pollock's career may be of great significance. At present it is not nearly as common for Canadian dramatists to work in a variety of media as it is for example in Great Britain (think of Harold Pinter, David Mercer and Trevor Griffiths). With the advent of Pay-Television another avenue has opened up. It is to be hoped that Sharon Pollock's out-of-court settlement with the production company adapting *Blood Relations* for Pay-TV will have the effect of ensuring that further ventures of this kind will respect the playwright's contribution. In the following remarks, then, I am not doing justice to her work as a whole.

Yet even an incomplete overview reveals a great deal about Sharon Pollock's strengths as a playwright; a pattern begins to take shape, the path she is taking begins to define itself.

A Compulsory Option, Sharon Pollock's first play, was written in 1971 and first produced in 1972. It is a lightweight farce about the funny side of the paranoia of the New Left, represented by a young man who is convinced that his one act of rebellion – he protested against the college cafeteria's serving blancmange five times in a row – has put him on the hit list of "the big money boys." He shares a flat with two other men: one he talks into sharing his suspicions; the other is the perfect object to project all this paranoia on, since he is a "raging queen," and the other two are loudly homophobic, and since he spends most of the play offstage, either in the bathroom meditating or in the hospital recovering from a gunshot wound he receives while tied to a chair. Hidden in this slightly ugly farce are elements that will be explored seriously in the later plays: the force exerted by oppressive institutions on individuals, discrimination against minorities, the power of myth.

Walsh first brought Sharon Pollock national attention. It was produced in Calgary in 1973 and the following year at Stratford. It has been in print for ten years now, and has worn well, although more as a play to read than as a play to perform. What keeps it fresh is its passion and sincerity and its ability to arouse troubling thoughts about Canada's treatment of aboriginal people and about its relations with the United States.

The impressive heart of the play is the encounter of Sitting Bull, chief of the Hunkpapa Sioux, and James A. Walsh, superintendent of the NWMP, two men of great dignity and integrity, who achieve a mutual respect that crosses a great racial and cultural divide. It chronicles how these men join the thousands of victims of the romantic myth of The Opening of the West, which casts the Indians as villains, the whites as heroes, and is utterly impervious to the truth. Walsh is forced, indeed, to become part of the ugly real-life destruction of aboriginal people which the myth rationalizes. The legend of General Custer, "flower of the American Army," proves to be stronger than the reality of his exterminatory raids, the retribution which caught up with him at Little Big Horn, the Sioux' exemplary behavior during the four years they stay in Canada, and Walsh's struggle to acquaint his government with the facts. Walsh, haunted through the play by Custer's marching song, "Garryowen," is pressed into the service of a fantasy cynically subscribed to by the Canadian government in order to maintain good relations with its mad neighbour to the south.

Walsh, imagining that he serves a government that bases its Indian policy on recommendations from the field, is brought face to face with the truth that he is a puppet and the Sioux are pawns, and that there is no justice or even sense to the policy he is obliged to carry out. When he breaks, he does so in the only way possible for a man of his integrity, by brutally, physically, acting out the cruelty hidden in the Prime Minister's directives. At the cost of both his and Sitting Bull's self-respect he strikes him and sends him sprawling. The moment is of a sort that seems to fascinate Sharon Pollock, for variations on it occur in most of her plays. After slamming the door so finally, or finding it slammed shut, on the way you have lived up to that moment, even on the very principles you have lived by, how do you go on from there?

The answer in *Walsh* is the powerful anti-climax which concludes the play. Walsh returns to his post after an extended leave (the audience having been kept in suspense in the meantime), quite willing to substitute the myth of the savage Indian for the reality he knew firsthand, to substitute "style," "show" and "image" for substance; he illustrates his plan to stage a mock-attack, Indian style, on Eastern dignitaries arriving to open the new railway, with toy soldiers mounted on a model: a precise metaphor for the state he has been reduced to. The plan is derailed by the news of the abject end of Sitting Bull at the hands of the United States Army. Walsh's helpless rage and grief at the news intensify the pathos of his surrender.

The play resorts to some awkward tactics to set this action up so that it will be viewed from the proper angle. The prologue, a flash-forward to the end of Walsh's career, is necessary so that we will understand from the start that his spirit will suffer destruction; the cynical Harry's long account of Custer's raids and his death at Little Big Horn is necessary to utterly demolish the legend of Custer, so that the audience will possess the ironic awareness of its persistence regardless of the facts; scene after scene in the first act are required to establish Walsh as a man of integrity sympathetic to the native people; a long scene in Sitting Bull's teepee is necessary to introduce the audience to the Way of the Medicine Wheel . . . But the result of all this is that the first half of the play sinks under the weight of exposition.

Pollock's interest in montage as a principle of composition first appears in *Walsh,* not completely successfully.

The juxtaposition of scenes in different styles seems partly due to a need to get certain things into the play, at least in the first act. Act II is much more successful at making montage contribute to the total effect, mainly because there is a much stronger through-line to carry us forward from scene to scene. For example, two scenes in very different styles – prosaic with Walsh, poetic with Sitting Bull – place the exhaustion of the two leaders in piquant contrast, and prepare for the climactic scene in which they confront each other for the last time.

Finally, in contrast to Pollock's later writing, the dialogue is such that every character means only what he says. There is no unverbalized subtext enriching, contradicting or counterpointing the text, as there is in her later work. Hence characterization is emphatically two-dimensional. What we see is what we get.

The Komagata Maru Incident (first produced in 1976) goes one layer farther down. Where *Walsh* set the myth of "Openin' the West" side by side with its dreadful acting out, this play goes after the myth of racial superiority that "Openin' the West" rested on, again by contrasting the rhetoric, "the clearly defined conception of moral necessity," "the Gift of Responsibility," with the dirty work involved in acting it out on real people.

Its protagonist's dilemma is more intimately reflective of its theme than was the case in *Walsh*. Walsh's integrity simply ran counter to the policy of his government. Inspector William Hopkinson of the Immigration Department identifies his integrity with his government's racist immigration policy and takes great pride in carrying it out. His conflict is with himself, for, as the play gradually reveals, his mother was a native of the Punjab. His racism is practised only through constant and strenuous denial of a part of himself. The through-line of the play – the slow return of the repressed – is more intriguing than that in *Walsh* where we indignantly watched "them" destroying that fine man (make that "us"). Here Hopkinson's anguish takes us farther into ourselves: the racist denies a part of his own humanity in denying the humanity of others.

The plot unfolds eerily, setting the ultimately successful effort of the Department of Immigration to prevent the landing of a boatload of Sikhs against Hopkinson's ultimately unsuccessful effort to suppress the Asian half of his inheritance.

It is an interesting process. Evy, Hopkinson's mistress, witnesses a Sikh being beaten by whites as she rides past in a streetcar, is horrified, and refuses to accept Hopkinson's comforting rationalization: "That's why we're sending the Komagata Maru back, so things like your fight won't happen." She confronts him soon after with his mother's race. He breaks down and begs her abjectly to stop. But the wall is breached. We have already seen his racism in the context of a number of hints of the force of his ambivalence – his contempt for Indians and his admiration for their workmanship, his refusal to be drawn out about his mother, his obsession with the woman and child aboard the Komagata Maru, his habit of disguising himself as a Sikh and going to the temple, the intense scene in which he recalls an encounter with an Indian in an empty bazaar the day after British soldiers had put down a disturbance there: "He stopped in the shadow of the huts ... he extended his arms t'wards me ... and I ... turned around ... and ran home." Hopkinson had seen his other self.

After Evy has breached the wall, his prosecution of his duties becomes strangely self-defeating. We see a partial enactment, partial narration, of his attempt to board the Komagata Maru from a sea-going tug. He has forgotten that the ship has a cargo of coal. He and his men are driven from the ship: he is struck down by a lump of coal – he looks like a chimney sweep. Through a neurotic oversight the meticulous civil servant has placed himself where he will be overwhelmed by the dark-skinned men in whom he refuses to see himself, until his skin too is dark. As he suffers the slow return to life of his buried self, his authority erodes and his superiors' approval dries up. He is finally left face to face with the Sikh who has come to assassinate him, and meets his death with an oriental resignation, quoting from a hymn to Shiva the Destroyer.

The structure of the play is an interesting montage of violently clashing styles: the naturalism of the scenes in Hopkinson's unofficial headquarters, the brothel, the gradually increasing poetic eloquence of the Sikh woman's interjections, the raucous carnival mood of the Master of Ceremony's spiels and impersonations of various government officials. The latter style, which frames the action and frequently erupts into it, has the disturbing effect of transforming an incident of brutal injustice into a sideshow complete with crudely obvious tricks of sleight-of-hand, imposing on the audience the role of idly curious passers-by. The problem of exposition, which loomed so large in *Walsh,* is neatly overcome here by being dashed off by the Master of Ceremonies with a briskness which is itself a harsh comment on the ugliness of the incident.

Sweet Land of Liberty, broadcast on CBC Soundstage in December 1979, has to be considered even in a brief survey of Sharon Pollock's dramatic writing. It is a very accomplished piece of radio drama (it was awarded a Nellie the following year) and an intriguing variation on her central theme. Its protagonist is an American who served his country proudly in Vietnam, suffered and did such terrible things there that he was driven to desert. His wanderings since then have finally taken him to a provincial park on the Alberta-Montana border; from a cliffside covered with petroglyphs he can see the homeland from which he is exiled. The play moves through an intricate montage of flashbacks within flashbacks to his suicide.

He is on the far side of the sort of crisis that destroyed Walsh and Hopkinson. What he was and what he served have pulled him apart. He is "strange," and what is strange about him is that he has ceased to live yet is still alive. Like Hopkinson walking through Vancouver towards his assassin, Tom perceives everything with uncanny clarity and detachment (he describes his ultra-patriotic sister in terms of her house – it has sharp edges you could cut yourself on, there is a little American flag in the window, and inside there is an organ anyone can play after ten lessons). The pathos of the tormented spirit in extremity receives its most intense expression in this work.

Blood Relations (first produced in 1980) is the first of the three plays published in Pollock's most recent volume. It is the best of the three, as its numerous productions across Canada testify. The best way to indicate its excellence is to point out that it is the most necessarily theatrical of all Sharon Pollock's plays. *Blood Relations* treats performance not as a vehicle for conveying something else but as an activity that by its nature may lead players and audience to revelations that it has literally brought into being.

The "game" is a development of a favourite device of the playwright, framing the action. In one form or another it appears in *Walsh, The Komagata Maru Incident* and *One Tiger to a Hill*. Here it is more than frame; it is completely integrated into the action as its very life. The play begins and ends in Lizzie Borden's parlor ten years after the axe-murder of her parents. She is entertaining her guest and lover, a professional actress. The latter urges Lizzie to confess. Did she or didn't she? Miss Lizzie presents her with a challenge: to paint the background by playing the role of Lizzie ten years back, and so come to her own conclusions. Miss Lizzie herself plays Bridget, the Irish maid, and the two bring the events of ten years ago back to life. The play is written in such a way that we never lose sight of the "real" characters during this role-playing. Bridget's feistiness is distinctly Lizzie-ish. And more importantly, she is constantly present, watching, cueing the actress-as-Lizzie, guiding her – in a word directing her. In fact the first 1892 scene, between Bridget and Harry, is a brilliant pastiche of the retrospective exposition of the opening of an Ibsen play, as if to say, "you're an actress, you'll understand this."

For the Actress, the game starts off as a great giggle – saying unladylike words, dishonouring her stepmother, correctly interpreting "Bridget's" reproaches as a cue to keep it up. But the game grows more and more serious as it goes along. As she begins to feel the oppressive atmosphere of the Borden home, as she feels more and more caged, she is guided by "Bridget" into rejecting one way out after another until there is only one way left. At strategic intervals, Miss Lizzie steps out of character and does what a good director does: she fills the actress's mind with images to guide her performance at the subconscious level. This is the function of the haunting description of the dream of a mask-like face with black holes for eyes, of the description of the puppy starved by its mother because it was different, *etc.* Playing Lizzie has gradually turned from a lark into a claustrophobic nightmare.

In the game, Miss Lizzie has complete control of the Actress, painting the background in such a way that the Actress chooses step by step to go on the strange winding path that leads to murder. Early on in the game, Miss Lizzie inserts two confessions, the first, that she was thirty-four yet still day-dreamt, the second that she feels as though she had been born defective without benefit of the magic formula for being "a woman." The Actress's emphatic reactions in effect are commitments to playing the role of Lizzie in a certain way whose consequences she cannot foresee. First: "thirty-four is too old to day-dream" means rejecting one way out of Lizzie's plight. Second: to insist that Lizzie is not defective is to rule out another form of resignation; it is to say on her behalf, I am normal and I want my freedom. Having made these choices, the Actress plays the confrontation with Lizzie's father and stepmother with unrestrained passion, and as Miss Lizzie well knows, is in no mood to accept the way out offered by "Bridget," in her story of the cook who secretly spat in her employers' soup. Another door has been slammed shut. Immediately, several more shut in quick succession: "I could / No. / I could / No. / I could / No!"

Following Miss Lizzie's hypnotic account of her dream of the mask and the scene that climaxes with her father's axe-murder of the birds, the Actress is face to face with the horrible imagining of murder. At the beginning of the second act there is an intense scene in which Lizzie pleads with her sister to stay and join forces with her to prevent the loss of their inheritance, the only hope of independence either of them has. What gives the scene its urgency is the Actress's foreknowledge that if Lizzie is left to stand alone, there are only two choices left, suicide or murder. The struggle between the two choices gives the second act its uncanny intensity. Miss Lizzie's climactic bit of stage directing is evident in the Actress's lines: "I want to die . . . I want to die, but something inside won't let me . . . inside something says *no*." The slightest touch from Miss Lizzie at this moment is crucial and is all that is necessary. After shutting her eyes, the Actress opens them to say "I can do anything," and from that point, murder is no longer fantastical, and everything that passes between Lizzie and her family is loaded with confirmation after confirmation that murder is all that is left.

The ending does not simply return us to 1902; the two players return with the unexpected and profoundly troubling recognitions that they both arrive at from having played the game. The Actress learns not only that her friend could have hacked two people to death, but – in the last line of the play that she herself could kill. Miss Lizzie, having just manoeuvred her alter-ego through a series of seemingly free choices, having just made someone else act out her life, is suddenly face to face with her elder sister and has a horrifying moment of self-estrangement, in which she sees herself as the someone else, and her sister as the manipulator: "your hand working my mouth, me saying all the things you felt like saying, me doing all the things you felt like doing." Two protagonists, two recognitions, crossing each other. The Actress can imagine killing to be the free woman she is now. Lizzie must ask herself: Am I, was I, free? Was I a puppet? A strange and haunting conclusion. The audience too is forced in these final moments to look back over the whole play with fresh eyes.

The ending makes the play a more dangerous confrontation and moves it away from being simply a sermon against the subjection of women, which is what the 1892 scenes would amount to if played by themselves, as indeed they were in the first version of the play, titled *My Name Is Lisbeth* (produced in 1976). One's response can then be quite comfortable: "look what an independent, spirited woman was driven to in 1892."

Surround these events with the "game" and you overlay their relatively acceptable message with disquieting insights into the mystery and ambiguity of personal identity: where do we draw the boundary between "me" and "not-me," on the near or far side of murder, on the near or far side of another person? In this context, the feminism of the play has a flavour of Pirandello. Being a woman is being the Other in somebody else's perceptions.

The play is also notable for the strength of its writing. The script is virtually uncuttable. The dialogue is spare and laconic but rich in subtext. Also new in Sharon Pollock's work is the metaphorical density, made possible here by the doubleness of the plot, where every object and gesture of 1892 is being searched for revelation in 1902, and by the complete assimilation of poetic passages into the structure of the play, something that wasn't quite carried off in earlier plays. Eyes, poison, birds, animals, recur through the script; it is also filled with the found metaphors of naturalism: the cage, the hatchet, staircase, money, newspaper, coffee and so on.

Blood Relations is a further development of a basic theme: a struggle to the breaking point between personal integrity and a larger force that denies it. Here there is an equivocal triumph. Lizzie does not break, she survives: how intact is the question. The oppressive force is no longer an identifiable institution or a consciously-undertaken program; the myth that sustains it needs no apologist. It is a patriarchal system so pervasive, so much the air everyone breathes, that Lizzie's struggle to break free of it seems mad and absurd. The father is a fascinating study of a man who is not even aware of an impermeable barrier in his mind between his affection for his daughter and the assumptions on which he bases his actions. Without abandoning the public dimension characteristic of her earlier plays, Sharon Pollock has shifted the accent; we now see the issue as it is reflected in the individual consciousness, from which vantage point we see beyond it and beneath it.

The montage-structure, characteristic of much of her work, is further developed in this play. The juxtaposition of 1892 and 1902 scenes has a compelling inner logic, as we have seen. The play's rhythm is an exacting challenge to performers. Act I's steadily-accelerating rhythm must successfully fuse with the gradually intensifying stillness of Act II.

One Tiger to a Hill, the second play in the volume, seems to me the least successful of Sharon Pollock's published plays. Although, like most of her plays, it is based on real events, in this case the famous riots in the British Columbia Penitentiary and at Attica Prison, it is curiously detached from reality, its characters and situations too close to the clichés of television melodrama.

The play unfolds as if narrated by a character much like Walsh, a lawyer whose faith in the system he serves is shaken to its roots by what he discovers when he finds himself inside the Pen as a mediator between hostagetakers and prison authorities. But his part in the action is so peripheral that it will not bear the weight of the anguish he informs us he is suffering. Like many things in the play – the rehabilitation work which we are told is held in contempt by the prison security staff, and the evil of solitary confinement which we do not get to hear about in any detail until near the end – it has to be taken on faith.

The most severe problem in the play is that the jarring clash between the political and the personal aspects of the play confuses rather than illuminates. The political message, conveyed by the rapid montage of scenes with the hostage-takers and with the prison authorities, carries depressing sense of hopelessness about changing the system, or even heading off a violent end to the crisis. But the violent end, in which two people are killed, arises out of pure soap opera. Has Dede, the classification officer, allowed Tommy, the ex-contract killer, to make love to her? When Tommy makes himself an easy target for Hanzuk, the guard, is he doing it to save Dede, whom he intended to use as a shield, or is he throwing his life away in despair over Dede's eleventh-hour confession that she does not love him? Does Hanzuk shoot Dede because he used to stand outside her office when Tommy was with her, seething with sexual hangups? All these possibilities are raised, quite insistently, and are all left up in the air; yet no other reading of the climactic events, particularly the death of Dede, is offered.

This sexual triangle imposes the stock motivations of melodrama onto a play that apparently intended to say something about the inhumanity of the prison system, particularly the arbitrary power and absence of due process pointed to by a character who does a lot of editorializing. In this play the personal and public aspects do not reinforce or resonate with each other, as they do in the other two plays in the volume. It is a confused and unfocused play, which has never worked on stage, except when Sharon Pollock herself directed a workshop production at the National Arts Centre.[3] Perhaps she directed the play she intended to write.

Generations, the third play in the volume, registers a further stage in a gradual shift of accent in Pollock's works from big issues to the characters on whom (and within whom) these issues have their impact. It is not at all a matter of dropping her concern with large social issues – certainly in *Generations* the impact of government policy on the survival of the family farm on the prairies is big enough. It is a matter of an almost Chekhovian approach, letting the texture of people's lives speak indirectly about the forces affecting them.

The dialogue has a refreshingly unportentous ring to it. Much more is said subtextually in this play than is the case with her previous work to 1980, even *Blood Relations,* where this kind of textured writing first appears (and is appropriately called "painting the background").

For instance, the opening sequence, an exchange between Old Eddy Nurlin and his grandson David, has a marvellous off-hand kind of humour, and accomplishes a considerable task of exposition at the same time. It conveys the strong sense of family, the sense of changing values over three generations, the strong bond between Old Eddy and David, on which the plot hinges, and concise and very vivid thumbnail sketches of the major characters and what Old Eddy thinks of them by way of pungent comments on their drinking habits.

The play focuses on two brothers, David and Young Eddy, and on the contrast between Young Eddy's leaving the farm to become a lawyer, and David's apparently fatalistic acceptance of the burden of being the third generation of Nurlins to run the place. To David's fiancée, Eddy seems a free person and David a person who will never have the chance to be what he wants. But the play is about inheritance, about how you can inherit an obligation that slowly ripens into a vocation, and about the family farm as not just a way of growing food but as a way of preserving a sense of a life spanning generations, indeed as a human construct that is bigger than the individual and so permits him to hold his own against the vastness of the prairie landscape. It is a difficult theme to dramatize, as the acceptance is fundamentally inarticulate, a product of time not of purposive action.

The play comes close to succeeding, although Sharon Pollock notes that none of the productions of the play has successfully met the enormous and maybe impossible task it imposes on a designer. The play calls for the most detailed farm-kitchen realism yet at the same time for the most abstract and mythic rendering of the prairie landscape. When the naturalistic dialogue reaches toward that mythic level, there is a similar clashing of gears. Still, even though the play is not completely successful, it does strike out into new territory. This is particularly evident in the climax. David is under the kind of pressure that Sharon Pollock always puts her protagonists under. His integrity and personal dignity are under attack from a number of directions – his brother, his fiancée, the faceless government representatives – and he finally erupts into the kind of irrevocable act we have seen in her previous plays. What do you do after you have burned the place down? But here the accent is entirely different. A thunderstorm douses the fire, Old Eddy gives David a "lickin" and tells him not to do that again. So the big moment is a throwaway. The stress is on the texture of life before the crisis and on how life is resumed afterwards. David emerges – not changed – but confirmed in what he knew already but could not articulate.

Sharon Pollock's radio play, *Intensive Care,* broadcast on CBC Radio in June 1983, is her most recently produced work.[4] It addresses the issue of euthanasia, yet goes beyond the limits of the issue. It explores the territory opened up by *Blood Relations,* the disquieting revelations at the boundaries of personal identity. In it, a nurse, who has made what seemed to her the sane and reasonable decision to pull the plug on a brain-dead patient, is horrified to discover that she has breached the boundaries that until then had restrained a fellow-nurse, who kills a hydrocephalic child because it would not have much of a life anyway, and attempts to take the life of an elderly man simply because he is a pain in the ass. The play ends with protagonist insisting with mounting anxiety that "there is a difference between her and me."

An overview of Sharon Pollock's work corrects the impression often conveyed in reviews that she is a didactic playwright whose characters are merely mouthpieces for social criticism. It is a conception framed with some justification on the basis of *Walsh,* and like many another journalistic ready-made, it clings to life. But ten years down the road it is clear that this stereotype has become increasingly ill-fitting. The grain of truth in it is her steady attention to the impact of public issues, and public myths, on individual lives. John Palmer's marvellous tirade, "Henrik Ibsen on the Necessity of Producing Norwegian Drama" (*CTR* 1977), implied that there was no reason why Canada could not produce a playwright of Ibsen's stature, as long as it undertook not actively to prevent such an occurrence. When Canada's answer to Ibsen emerges, it will be someone like Sharon Pollock, with her long-haul commitment to the discipline, with her experimentation, and expansion of the boundaries of her dramatic universe, and quite possibly with her practise of working in more than one performance medium.

Notes

1. I would like to thank Gail Donald, of CBC Program Archives in Toronto, for permitting me to listen to a number of tapes of Sharon Pollock's radio plays. Difficulties with Canada Post have so far sabotaged Sharon Pollock's kind effort to let me read scripts of her other two produced but unpublished full-length plays: *And Out Goes You?* (first produced in 1975) and *Whiskey Six* (first produced in 1983). For a comprehensive checklist of Sharon Pollock's work to 1980, see *Canada's Playwrights: A Biographical Guide*, eds. Don Rubin and Allison Cranmer-Byng, Downsview, Ont: Canadian Theatre Review Publications, 1980.
2. Malcolm Page discusses this earlier version in his article in *Canadian Drama/L'Art dramatique Canadien*, 5.2 (Fall 1979): 104-111.
3. See Audrey M. Ashley's review in the *Ottawa Citizen*, 23 March 1981.
4. This article was written before the production by Theatre Calgary in March 1984 of her new play, *Doc*.

Works Cited

Pollock, Sharon. *Blood Relations and Other Plays*. Edmonton: NeWest Press, 1981.

Pollock, Sharon. *A Compulsory Option*. Unpublished: Script available from the New Play Centre, Vancouver.

Pollock, Sharon. *Intensive Care*. CBC, 1983.

Pollock, Sharon. *The Komagata Maru Incident*. Toronto: Playwrights Canada, 1978.

Pollock, Sharon. *Sweet Land of Liberty*. CBC, 1979.

Pollock, Sharon. *Walsh*. Vancouver: Talonbooks. Stratford, Ontario version, 1973.

Sharon Pollock's Women

A Study in Dramatic Process

Diane Bessai

At a summer 1985 conference in Toronto on women's issues in the theatre, Rina Fraticelli cited playwright Sharon Pollock (along with the American Joanne Akalaitis and British Caryl Churchill) as representing "the distinct female viewpoint" that in her estimation would eventually "transform the (male) esthetic code that has dominated Western Culture" (Conlogue S13). Pollock herself resists the ideological label of "feminist" along with any other that restricts her artistic independence (Bessai, "Women" 41). However, since her plays from *Blood Relations* (1980) to the present show increasing attention to feminine individuality, Fraticelli's appropriation of Pollock as a feminist playwright might bear closer examination. Perhaps a feminist *manqué* is emerging from the wings, or more to the point what is taken for feminism is an aspect of this playwright's on-going response to new dramaturgical challenges: what critic Malcolm Page regarded in 1979 as Pollock's "restless determination to avoid obvious approaches and search for angles which are effective and unusual" (100).

While her continuing experimentation with dramatic styles and structures may seem to fit Fraticelli's conception of radical feminist dramaturgy, in this regard Sharon Pollock should also be numbered among the several new playwrights and playmakers beginning to write in the early 1970s, all of whom were challenging the conventions of theatrical aesthetics in their determination to establish a native drama.[1] In her earlier plays of commitment to public and social concerns, Pollock in her Canadian context was actually closer to what British feminist critic Michelene Wandor has identified as the male-oriented stream of radical social theatre in the Britain of the period as opposed to the personal focus of the feminist (7). Thus what makes Pollock's plays of the 1980s attractive to feminists should be examined in relation to her whole growth as a playwright, a growth that can indeed be explored through her approach to female characterization and feminine themes, but within the broader range of her thematic intentions and structural explorations.

In her first plays Pollock is offering perspectives on historical events that she finds directly related to contemporary problems: *Walsh* (1973) locates abuse of indigenous peoples in the expedient policies of the Macdonald government of the 1870s; *The Komagata Maru Incident* (1976) identifies contemporary racism against Asians in the self-protective legislation of the era before World War I. Canadians, she asserts, "have this view of themselves as nice civilized people who have never participated in historical crimes and atrocities . . . But that view is false. Our history is dull only because it has been dishonestly expurgated" (Hofsess T03). During this period she is also a confrontational voice on contemporary issues: in the comic handling of a housing expropriation incident, her political satire *Out Goes You* (1975) explores the failure of the modern political Left to distinguish itself from the Right; *One Tiger to a Hill* (1979) speaks of the injustice and cruelty of penal institutions. The political and social anger are strong in these plays, each with its different mode of expressive theatricality.

The women of *Walsh* and *The Komagata Maru Incident* function largely as devices to reveal the public conflicts of central male characters, to the minor degree of their slight appearance in the former, more pointedly in the latter. The two women characters of *One Tiger to a Hill*, although more firmly grounded within the conflict of the play, essentially are intended as two of several points of view within the play's ethical argument. There is a turning point in this regard with *Blood Relations*, Pollock's Lizzie Borden play, with its entirely feminine point of view, the one that the playwright concedes to be "feminist." Further, through its unusual manipulation of a play-within-a-play structure, this work subsumes its issues entirely within personal character conflicts. *Blood Relations*, therefore, may be judged both the culmination of Pollock's polemical phase and the anticipation of her later directions: a shift noted by Robert Nunn "from big issues to the characters on whom . . . these issues have their impact" ("Sharon Pollock's Plays" 81). With the changed emphasis from public to domestic worlds in the plays of the 1980s – *Generations* (1981), *Whiskey Six Cadenza* (1983), *Doc* (1984) – women play crucial although still not necessarily central roles.

Like several of her Canadian contemporaries, Sharon Pollock initially served an apprenticeship to documentary drama. This is reflected not only in her researched subject matter but also in her informational dramatic techniques aimed at direct audience engagement with the facts of the particular issue at hand. For Pollock the challenge was to forge documentation into a dramatic shape that neither restricts the argument emerging from the facts nor reduces characterization to cipher. Reflecting the belief that "theatre should hit people emotionally" while making its critical social or political point, each of her factually based plays to 1980 marks a fresh effort towards the integration of investigational and psychological realities. Her various experiments with presentational stage narration are the measure of her progress in handling documentation as persuasive on-stage information; her specific use of female characterizations reflects her increasing efforts to "personalize" the issues representationally.

In the original version of *Walsh*, the episodic chronological structure of the play combined semi-fictionalized dramatic scenes (depicting Major James Walsh's increasing conflict with his N.W.M.P. superiors on the matter of the continuing presence of Sitting Bull's Sioux in Canada) and anonymous voice-over delivery of the historical documentation of government policy during these years. In its revised version of the following year, *Walsh* now absorbed its documentary function (what Pollock thought of as explaining the facts [Allen 31]) into a narrating character as authenticating voice. By the time of *The Komagata Maru Incident*, she was disclaiming the "documentary" label in favour of "a theatrical impression" of the historical facts, explaining to an interviewer before the premiere that for the audience "to learn and understand, the people of the situation must be put across. A barrage of documented data gets in the way." Here a confrontational narrating voice, T.S., the "Master of Ceremonies" of the whole "racist sideshow" (Allen 31) that comprises the play, takes on a dramatic relation to the audience by addressing it throughout as "an idly curious crowd" that tacitly condones such events (Nunn, "Performing Fact" 55). As well as carrying the documentary burden of the incident, T.S. also stage manages the personal scenes of the play and himself serves as a multipurpose authority figure when the plot requires. Under his direction public and personal scenes inter-cut in rapid cinematic succession what one reviewer identified as "jump-cut, fast-freeze, time-slip TV style of construction" (Wyman 43).

The personal dimension of the play is primarily conducted from a peripheral perspective to the main events: the setting for this is a seedy brothel from which William Hopkinson, head of intelligence for the Department of Immigration, conducts spying operations against the Vancouver Sikhs who are trying to facilitate the landing of the passengers from the Komagata Maru. At the same time Hopkinson is also conducting an affair with Evy, the madam of the place. She, her associate Sophie, and Sophie's client, the German Georg Braun, become key figures in the behind-scenes action. Life on board the ship is conveyed from the perspective of a third woman, a Sikh mother who is represented at intervals consoling her frightened child during the six-week ordeal of awaiting admission into a country that only theoretically accepts British citizens of whatever origin.

Hopkinson's private racial conflicts are at the heart of this play, the three women serving to reveal the nature and consequences of the incident to him personally. Initially he is seen as a brash authoritarian who relishes his orders to deny the Sikhs entry. Unlike the earlier Walsh, who confronts his superiors on matters of principle and practice, Hopkinson is toady to his. His moral viciousness is further underlined by his exploitation of Evy's establishment against her will. She herself is the stereotypically good-hearted whore who has sympathy for the plight of the would-be immigrants. She also senses that Hopkinson's racism may have a hidden cause in his own ambiguous racial background. He likes to give the impression that his first-hand knowledge of India (his father was a

British army officer there and he himself was in the Lahore police) lends authority to his avowals of the superiority of Europeans. Although Evy is powerless to influence Hopkinson's thinking about the Komagata Maru passengers (she has seen a Sikh abused in an employment lineup, an incident she pityingly connects with the predicament of the 376 people in the harbour), she does begin to undermine his certainties in her mocking probings of his childhood in India. In confronting him with her suspicion that his own mother was a Sikh, she becomes the instrument for revealing Hopkinson as a divided man: in rejecting the Sikhs, he is rejecting a part of himself. (His mixed blood, in fact, is being exploited by his superiors.)

That Hopkinson has chosen his side but cannot entirely live with it is further indicated by his response to the Woman and her child on the ship. They haunt him to the degree that he countervenes orders to deny supplies. Later, in a skirmish between the Immigration party and the passengers, he hopes that the Woman and child see him unflinching as the passengers are hurling lumps of coal at the officials; ironically he is hit, knocked down and blackened by a missile the Woman throws (Pollock 37). By the end of the play, she has become politicized against the blatant injustice of imperialist rule.

While Sophie's function is less precise to the characterization of Hopkinson than the other two, she is a specific example of the racist ambience to which the master of ceremonies is constantly drawing attention; her interest in the sensationalism confirms her own bigotry. In this play the women figures, although stereotypical and two dimensional as characterizations, are the playwright's chief device for providing moral perspective to events as well as for contributing to the emotional dimension centred in the character of Hopkinson (who eventually dies at the hand of a Sikh assassin in retributive justice).

In the play as a whole, however, the problem of trying to make the personalization of issues work within a presentational political structure is not resolved. For one thing, the potentially tragic figure of Hopkinson is a special case rather than a typically motivated example of racist thinking. The more compelling the playwright attempts to make his particular conflict, the more intrusive seem the facts and figures of the sardonic T.S. who is the voice of the system she is attacking, and through whom she invites the audience to self-judgement. The constant interruptions by the narrating figure both truncate and intrude on the development of the personal fable and its ironies. Contradictorily the play is directed away from the public domain in terms of its political message. In this work, as in a different way in *One Tiger to a Hill,* Pollock's desire to move her audience emotionally is at war with her equal desire to engage them politically.

While *The Komagata Maru Incident* establishes clear polarities between justice and injustice within the law, *One Tiger to a Hill* tries to offer multiple perspectives on legalized violence. This play is roughly based on the New Westminster penitentiary hostage-taking of 1975 in which a classification officer, Mary Steinhauser, was shot to death by an unidentified member of the prison's tactical squad. Recent comments by Pollock reveal that she originally intended to write the play from Steinhauser's point of view or "a character very much like her" (Wallace and Zimmerman 122). Instead the play is framed by the narrating voice of Ev Chalmers, a lawyer who inadvertently becomes a negotiator between the hostage-takers and the authorities. As a kind of middle-class Everyman, he personally absorbs the impact of events and of the complex institutional problems these manifest in relation to prisoners and staff alike. By creating an authenticating outside character with whom the audience can identify, Pollock is hoping to persuade the audience of the reality of "events that were just facts before" (Bessai, "Women" 41).

The inside perspective is to varying degrees personalized by characterizations of warden, security and rehabilitation officers and, of course, prisoners. In the play's ongoing debate on the question of "cruel and unusual punishment," each represents the point of view of his or her calling. The playwright appears to be striving for a certain documentary objectivity in her approach, although not documentary in the specific particulars of the New Westminster incident itself.[2] The work as a whole is a structurally fluid combination of discussion and suspenseful action set in the several key on-stage locations of the prison that, together, physically and symbolically identify prison hierarchy and its communication problems. Yet the polemical focus is only partially successful through the characters themselves.

Dede Walker is the catalyst of the hostage-taking incident and thereby central to its drama. An ardent believer in the reform of the prison rehabilitation system and herself the practitioner of highly personal counselling methods, her proud example of success is the hitherto incorrigible Tommy Paul. The rumour among security and administration is that she has sexual intercourse with Paul in her office. In fact, through the entire play it is never entirely clear whether sexism or sexuality is at issue against Walker, particularly as far as the guard Hansuk, who eventually shoots her, is concerned. This, compounded with the ambiguity in her own expression of feelings for Tommy Paul, points to a problem in the play, certainly as far as its multiple points of view are concerned. It is far too easy for the audience to sympathize uncritically with the young woman as well-intentioned victim, whether she is interpreted as courageous or merely foolish, and to attribute the burden of the play's message to her situation alone. That inclination is intensified by the tender exchanges between Dede and Tommy, whether implicitly expressing sexual or humanitarian love, or, more likely, both. The pragmatic voice of Frank Soholuk, Dede's colleague and fellow hostage, has less appeal, therefore, although as her critic he makes a certain sense. For example, he alerts her to the dangers in her personalist thinking when she refuses to assist in their one chance to over-power Tommy and his pathetic confederate Gilie Dermott. Soholuk's angry accusation that she is "a lamb looking for a slaughter," is a reasonable challenge to her unrealistic notion that Paul might do some good in his negotiations for the reforms she taught him to value. He is justified since innocent lives, his own included, are at stake and in this light Dede's self-defined "just cause" smacks of 1960s' love-in heroics (118).

The other woman character, Lena Benz, a salty old streetcorner radical, is universal friend to all victims of oppression whether in prison or on the picket lines. She has been brought in to co-negotiate with Ev Chalmers. If Dede suggests the cloudy thinking of the 1960s new left, Lena represents the failure of the old left as inherited from the 1930s. Despite her vigorous denunciation of the system to the warden, she has little to bring to the hostage-taking situation except a mess of cold "Kentucky fried" as a morale booster to the "boys." Privately she tells Ev that her way would be to "Put a torch to the place."[3] Lena is also an appealing character, comic in her forthrightness and in her unique propensity for breaking into prisons.

Unlike Dede, however, she is given inexplicable short shrift half way through the play, perhaps implying that rabble rousing is even more futile than humanitarian emotionalism.

Once more, as in *The Komagata Maru Incident* in the case of Hopkinson, personality is more a distraction than a reinforcement to the issues of the play. Nor is Pollock intending to defend her women characters over her men, although there is something brave in their head-on challenge to the system. This is a play in which no one wins, with the possible exception of Ev Chalmers in that he has become implicated in a world that hitherto, like "the good Germans" of the Nazi era, he had never questioned (Wallace and Zimmerman 121-2).

The play *Blood Relations,* in contrast to Pollock's previous work, was initiated from an interest in the dramatic possibilities of the story rather than an issue per se. She had written an earlier version in 1975 entitled *My Name Is Lisbeth*, as a naturalistic exercise reflecting her hobby interest in violent crime. The crime in this case is the famous axe murders of 1892 in which a New England spinster was charged and acquitted of the murder of her father and step-mother; although the crime was never solved, many writers have since reviewed the evidence on the matter of Lizzie's guilt. Pollock claims she was dissatisfied with her first play (in which Lizzie does commit the murders) because she lost interest in the who-done-it question. What attracted her more was the ambiguity that is now an inherent part of the Lizzie Borden myth. The re-structuring of the play into its present form (developed at a 1977 workshop at the playwright's colony in Banff) transforms basically the same events of *My Name Is Lisbeth* into a context that both exploits the ambiguity and introduces what Pollock has casually referred to as "a lot of women's lib numbers," adding: "In a way I found myself using an historical situation for a metaphor for a much more contemporary women's theme" (Ashwell D2). The difference from the other historically-based plays is *Blood Relations'* metaphoric rather than causal focus on the present, for which the vehicle is organically theatrical.

The new structure comprises a play-within-the-play performed in 1902, ten years after the murders. The performers are Miss Lizzie Borden herself, although she plays the role of Bridget the maid, and her friend the unnamed Actress in the role of Lizzie. In this "dream thesis" enactment of the two days leading to the murders, the other participants emerge in flash-back as required. The 1902 time frame permits the portrayal of Miss Lizzie's emotional relationship with the Actress, mostly made manifest in her "painting in the background" from time to time as the performance game proceeds. This allows Miss Lizzie the role of director, as it were, when she is not playing Bridget. This outer play is dramatically a more sophisticated development of the various presentational narrating devices Pollock hitherto attempted; in this case the Actress, like Ev Chalmers in *One Tiger to a Hill,* is the participating outsider in the process of discovering answers to important questions, but the Actress is more personally involved and in her case performance is her best method of expression.

Since the "affair" is based on the Actress's own fascination with the ambiguity, Miss Lizzie herself has no way of directly responding to her friend's inevitable question, "did you?", and so suggests the game. Ironically, the Actress, who starts out tentatively playing Lizzie under Miss Lizzie's guidance, by the second act has taken over the part so completely and convincingly that she has forgotten her friend in the intensity of her own performance. Indeed she seems to have forgotten that it *is* performance and so for a time she has become Lizzie Borden, or her own idea of her. When she recovers herself she is able to conclude, "Lizzie, you did." But finally Miss Lizzie refuses to acknowledge the Actress's version, even though she helped her friend to discover it. Instead she coolly answers with the literal truth of what she and the audience were on the verge of witnessing, saying "I didn't. You did" (70).

For Miss Lizzie to admit to any final self-recognition in her friend's performance would be to disturb her own carefully preserved present-day identity as the ambiguous Miss Lizzie Borden – particularly since the Actress's depiction explores the people and events of ten years ago in terms of the threatened violation *then* of Lizzie's sense of self. For example, Actress/Lizzie says to Mr. Borden, "I'm supposed to be a mirror. I'm supposed to reflect what you want to see, but everyone wants something different. If no one looks in the mirror, I'm not even there, I don't exist!" (39). In their piquantly co-operative effort, the substance of this idea is picked up and elaborated a little later by Miss Lizzie in one of her coaching speeches about a dream of seeing herself on a carousel wearing a mask with no eyes behind it. Eyes are also Miss Lizzie's link to the bright eyes of love she sees in her pet birds that her father kills with an axe, this in a fit of anger and guilt that concerns his transfer of Lizzie's cherished farm to the use of his wife's hateful brother. Ironically this is the same father whom Lizzie also deeply loves and who loves her when she is "good." Actress/Lizzie creates a divided person: the strong rebellious self at war with the vulnerable little girl self.

Through *Blood Relations'* playful structure, then, the historical situation becomes "a metaphor for a more contemporary women's theme." The contemporary theme is the identity question that interpenetrates the outer and inner play by means of the romantic relationship played out between the two women in the process of the performance: one is inviting intimacy while the other is trying to respond. The climax of that performance and its aftermath, noted above, has the additional and perhaps more important effect of revealing the feminist politic of the play. This is to say, in the playwright's own comment, that "all of us are capable of murder given the right situation" (Wallace and Zimmerman 121-2). In the context of the play as a whole, this is a feminist point. The "right circumstances" that support the Actress's interpretation of psychological violation are shaped by Pollock from the historical Lizzie Borden's life. She is a spinster who has no freedom of choice beyond whatever the oppressive conventions of her social class would allow in 1892: marriage or dutiful daughterhood. Ironically what probably saved her from the noose, as the voice of the Defence in *Blood Relations* makes clear, is the reversed sexism of disbelief that a "gentlewoman" who is "a recipient of the fullest amenities our society can bestow upon its most fortunate members" could be "capable of such an act" (36). By in effect reversing that point on the audience as well as the Actress, Pollock is forcing the realization that feminist questions have been asked without insisting on absolute answers, questions that have as much to do with the audience as with Lizzie Borden.[4]

In this play Sharon Pollock has most successfully achieved her aim to move the audience emotionally and yet distance it intellectually through what begins and concludes as a Brechtian performance (Bessai, "Theatre"

6). Formally and philosophically Pollock has virtually created an anti-documentary play; she has moved from a critical corrective to history (for example in *Walsh* and *The Komagata Maru Incident,*) to an implicit critique of documentary drama's basic assumption that the truth can be demonstrably discovered in an investigatory dramatic structure. What remains in *Blood Relations* is documentary's presentational strategy of interaction between investigation and reconstruction. In this case, however, the reconstruction itself is wittily suspect.

The questions about women's dependence and independence initiated in *Blood Relations* continue in the plays to follow. Women are still basically portrayed through their connections with men, but their personal perspectives are more individually articulated than before *Blood Relations:* there are those who have reasons to conform to the dominant male version of themselves and those who struggle against it. In *Whiskey Six Cadenza* and *Doc,* the male characters who are central to the drama are largely presented through their relationships with women, that is, in a dramatic way rather than in the structural relationship demanded by the issues of the earlier plays. As the imagination begins to free itself from documentation in Pollock's work – a sign in evidence throughout her earlier writing with mixed results – she becomes more introspective about human relations, continuing to strive for the unusual stage approach in a manner that combines old methods and themes with new.

In Pollock's next play, *Generations,* questions raised in *Blood Relations* on matters of dependence and identity are put directly into a modern context where, unlike Lizzie, one is free to choose. The main theme of the play (the only naturalistic stage work to date) is the tie of the land as it affects the three generations of Nurlin farmers from old

Eddie, the pioneer, to his grandson David who is expected to carry on the family tradition and shows every indication of wanting to do so. The woman's question enters through David's girl friend Bonnie, a local school teacher who is infected with rather undefined aspirations for a different way of life. If *Blood Relations* deals with the *condition* of female oppression, then *Generations* refers to its *prevention*. When Bonnie talks about fear of losing "herself" (although it is not too clear to her or the audience who that self is), all she has to do is walk away, which she does, in the belief that "this country uses people up and wears them out and throws them away!" and that for her, if she leaves, "There's worse things than [being] lonely" (170, 189).

She walks away, in effect, from the traditional life of the exploited and desperate farm women deplored by so many writers of prairie fictional realism from F.P. Grove and Sinclair Ross to Gwen Ringwood and Margaret Laurence. Pollock, however, also provides a twist to that prairie stereotype in the character of Margaret Nurlin, David's mother. She actually likes her life on the farm and has chosen it freely: when her own family lost everything to the Depression, she was glad to marry Alfred and "be part of something again" (189). Even though this also means that she is apt to acquiesce to the men's decisions (the current question is her eldest son's request for the sale of a section of land to finance his new law practice), she is still a more solidly articulated character than the rather nebulous Bonnie whose dividedness is realized perhaps more prescriptively than dramatically in the play. While Bonnie urges the same questions she asks of herself on David in his circumstance as the son who is expected to stay, his relationship to his grandfather and the land itself seems more relevant than his relationship to her. However, the point is only implicitly ironic.

In the second and more ambitious of her Alberta plays, *Whiskey Six Cadenza,* Pollock has better succeeded in the dramatic integration of her women characters in the male dominated world of its setting. Once again she has distanced herself from the present by examining a controversial era from the Canadian past, this time prohibition as it affects the small Crowsnest Pass mining town of Blairmore in 1919 and 1920. But in this case she shows no direct political concern to correct the distortions of history as with *Walsh* or *The Komagata Maru Incident;* nor is she ostensibly trying to free the story from the past in order to make it a present-day experience for the audience as in *Blood Relations.* While the same general public themes of earlier work are present, particularly how authoritarian regulation destroys freedom of choice and self-responsibility, this in its prohibition setting serves the fictional circumstances rather than an overt didacticism. Although the work was initially drawn from a documentary base (Brennan H1), the playwright has made her polemics the function of plot and character. *Whiskey Six Cadenza* is a haunting balladic fable of a curious and ultimately tragic love triangle that strives to retain its sense of pastness rather than insisting on a modern exposé of that past.

Johnny Farley, a naive young man whose father is a miner and whose mother is strict temperance, falls in love with an "incandescent" young woman, Leah, whose protector in the guise of foster-father is Mr. Big, the local rum-runner (and whose six-cylinder McLaughlin car, good for bootlegging getaways, gives the play its title). Originally conceived as a musical, the play retains something of that quality in its unobtrusive memory structure and its impressionist interweaving of musical and visual images; these both complement individual scenes and compositely create a pattern of the conflicting "multiple realities" that fatefully dominate the lives of the characters.

The ugliest of these are the shocking working conditions in the mines. Also, in these drab working lives, prohibition with its regulation two percent beer makes even the most obvious avenue of temporary escape difficult. The lively, often comic action of the play has to do with the clumsy efforts of Bill Windsor, of the Alberta prohibition police, to catch Mr. Big in his nefarious dealings in the bar of the Alberta Hotel. On the personal side is the apparent freedom of romantic reality: between Will, Johnny's older brother, and Dolly and, as the play develops, between Johnny and Leah. Johnny, at the express bidding of his mother, had sought to leave Blairmore and the mines behind, but now he has been forced to return for lack of work elsewhere. He alienates his mother by going to work for Mr. Big; to Mrs. Farley, liquor's danger to the soul is far worse than the mine's damage to the body. Further, there are nasty rumors about Mr. Big's ambiguous relationship to his "chosen daughter" Leah.

In the centre of it all is the larger-than-life character of the self-named Mr. Big himself. He is a man of generous and loving nature: to his wife, Mama George, to Johnny, and above all to Leah whom he rescued from the streets at the age of eleven, "like God descendin' to take his chosen up into Heaven in a fiery chariot." Mr. Big's characteristic speech is ripe with grandiloquent Bible Belt rhetoric, but his is the evangelism of free choice, making him the most voluble critic of prohibition, despite the inherent contradiction that it makes him a profitable living. He likes to denigrate government for its denial of the right of individual choice, insisting that "It's only when individuals choose and suffer the consequences that humanity can progress." Persuasive though this position might be in contrast to the sanctimonious thinking of Mrs. Farley, the deeper ramifications of Mr. Big's philosophy gradually show their dark and ironic side in his personal life; he translates everything that flatters his own sense of power over mundane human restraints into transcendent terms. At first Johnny is enthralled by his refreshing individuality, but more wary of his mentor's proud boast that as "a colossus bestriding my world" he has "mastered" the conflicting "multiple realities of the universe" especially when Leah seems the embodiment of that supposed omniscience.

Both the public and personal dimensions of *Whiskey Six Cadenza* turn on the theme of freedom of choice exemplified in the actions of Mr. Big. On the personal level the crux is his relationships to the women in his family and therein lies the essential drama of the play. Mama George has the same capacity for self-abnegation that Bonnie, in *Generations,* criticizes in Margaret Nurlin; but the extraordinary form it has taken, unbeknownst even to Mr. Big, is that out of love for him she has tacitly given him his freedom of choice concerning Leah. Leah herself, who also loves him, has an oddly innocent acquiescence to the circumstances she has never had cause to question openly until the advent of Johnny. In the process of becoming an independent person, Leah discovers that her own power of choice has been fatally limited. The irony is that Mr. Big must now accept the consequences of *his* choice and "make it right" for Leah in the only way she deems possible; it is *her* choice that he must take away the life he gave her.

The play concludes with Johnny elegiacally looking back from a later time and, like Ev Chalmers in *One Tiger to a Hill*, wondering which were the lies and which the truth. Indeed, although Mr. Big personally becomes the victim of his own philosophy, its opposite extreme is no more attractive for it, either in Mrs. Farley or Bill Windsor. However, in *Whiskey Six Cadenza*, the polarities of argument about the public jurisdiction of choice dissolve into the half-hidden complexities of sadly destructive personal relationships.

Personal relations are the continued subject of *Doc*, but in a new thematic dimension for Pollock in which the conflict lies between public and domestic responsibility, although with the focus on the latter. Ev is an aging doctor whose partially estranged daughter, Catherine, returns for a brief visit to the small Maritime city of her youth coincidentally on the eve of the dedication of a new hospital in his name. Through the play's recollection of that life from inside the family, Ev's successful dedication to community health seems almost entirely at the expense of his wife, Bob, and through her, his daughter Katie. Whereas in *Whiskey Six Cadenza* dramatic obliquity serves the ambiguity in the family relationships of Mr. Big, in *Doc* the conflicts are virtually politically polarized, emerging head on, tonally reminiscent of T.S.'s confrontations with the audience in *The Komagata Maru Incident*. Bob wants to return to nursing after Katie's birth; Ev would find this professionally awkward. Bob dislikes the social round of a doctor's wife; Ev is too busy with his patients to spare her enough time to compensate. Each is deaf to the other's point of view and in something hinting at a feminist perspective represented in the older Katie (now Catherine) the pattern of confrontation is set towards the inevitable disintegration of home life.

Not since *Blood Relations*, with its dramatically motivated linkage of the past to a fictional present, has Pollock devised so complex a structure for the dramatic handling of narrative point of view. In a further step from the retrospective time frame, *Doc* also rejects chronology: the past occurs in a multidimensional refraction from the present with fragmented memory images arising associationally from the minds of the two present-time characters, Ev and Catherine, who are both remembering and commenting on the family past. Catherine watches and reacts to her own on-stage younger self caught between a professionally pre-occupied father and an alcoholic mother. There is also a mediating memory character, Oscar, Ev's best friend and temperamental opposite. Ev, perhaps because a less introspective and divided person than his daughter, plays his own younger self.

The memory images that alternately fade and resurge throughout the play are more often heated accusatory moments than the fully articulated dramatized recollections of earlier plays. Here the years collapse into a swirl of dominant images of either words or actions. Dramatic progression is deliberately buried in the kaleidoscopic patternings of recurring character motifs within the scenes or fragments of scenes. This is facilitated by the presence of all the characters on stage throughout (the time montage, like *The Komagata Maru's* cinematic fragmentation of location, controlled by lighting), making the physical setting of the house (like *One Tiger's* prison) symbolic as much as representational of failed communication.

The general intent of the method is to engage the audience along with the present-time characters in the painful and difficult *experience* of remembering. This works up to a point, but the unrelieved confrontational matter and tone tend to polarize rather than to integrate the character motifs of the play. Catherine's contemporary response to her younger self relieves this to some degree (as do some scenes with the gentler Oscar). While she is shown still sharing Katie's personal guilts and fears about her mother and herself, she is also able to bring her adult feminine perspective to Ev's adamant response to Bob's need to continue her career and also to Bob's reticence about taking matters into her own hands.

The strong female perspective on Ev, while seldom defeating his professional sense of purpose, has much to do with the way the audience is forced to view him. On the one hand, as far as his wife is concerned (and possibly his daughter) he should be supplying answers to what he does not ever recognize as questions. In the feminine politic of the play this makes him out as an insensitive autocrat without insight or humanity concerning the problems that conventional social attitudes impose on individualistic women. On the other hand, as a physician he is impressively committed to the suffering poor with an approach to patients that is entirely personal. This makes him a dedicated humanitarian with a domestic blind spot that is never fully accounted for; this also puts him on the defensive throughout the whole course of the play.

The deepest irony, with which the play concludes, is not that Bob inevitably took her own life or that Katie/Catherine became estranged, but that Ev can finally wonder if his whole career of personal involvement with the well-being of his patients is finally worth it. Given his own present state of health, he is now face to face with the creeping impersonality of high tech developments in medicine that he, in his various crusades for facilities and expertise, helped to promote. In his profession he did ask the right questions and sought the right answers, but he has lived to see that profession transcend the personal approach he had always brought to his practice. This, he ruefully notes, is what has taken up his life.

As a play, although interesting in what it attempts through its complex dramatic structure, *Doc* is only partially satisfactory. It fails as a feminist play in its underdevelopment of the character of Catherine (as *Generations* did earlier in the case of Bonnie); it refuses to be a social issue play, except peripherally in the matter of Ev's humanitarian commitment, vivid though his accounts may be. There is no right or wrong side in *Doc*, although its confrontational tone within its domestic milieu leads one to expect there should be. But this play does demonstrate Pollock's ever-increasing capacity to master the complexities of her stage craft as the means of widening her range of dramatic subjects. It would be a mistake to impose categorical restrictions on her achievement to date. At some future time *Doc* may well seem the mark of a transitional phase in Sharon Pollock's *oeuvre* (as does *The Komagata Maru Incident* from this present), showing, perhaps, the playwright in the process of a further move toward the exploration of the personal intricacies of social and familial responsibility.

Notes

1. For example, Carol Bolt, Rick Salutin, Michael Cook, Rex Deverell, and the collective companies such as Theatre Passe Muraille, particularly in *The Farm Show*.
2. For a play closer to the facts of the incident, see Christina Bruyere, *Walls*.
3. Lena is an echo of "Goose," the old on-to-Ottawa trekker of *Out Goes You*. Awakened forty years after she was shot by the RCMP during the Regina riots, she incites her politically

diffident offspring to radical action. Lena, like Goose, is finally ineffective against modern forces of conservatism.

4 For the feminist drama critics who reject the absolute authority of the written text, the "inner script" of *Blood Relations* might have some appeal since it presents events as process rather than as absolute; it also makes clear distinctions between character and performance, although not to the same degree as does Caryl Churchill in *Cloud Nine.* See Ann Wilson.

WORKS CITED

Allen, Bob. "Play Reveals Shame of Komagata Maru." *The Vancouver Province,* 16 January 1976: 31.

Ashwell, Keith. "Playwright Pollock set to score with *Blood Relations.*" *The Edmonton Journal,* 11 March 1980: D2.

Bessai, Diane. "Theatre Provocateur." *NeWest Review,* 5.8 (April 1980): 6.

Bessai, Diane. "Women, Feminism and Prairie Theatre." *Canadian Theatre Review,* 43 (Summer 1985): 4.

Brennan, Brian. "Tourist pamphlet inspired new Pollock play." *Calgary Herald,* 6 February 1983: H1.

Bruyere, Christian. *Walls.* Vancouver: Talonbooks, 1978.

Conlogue, Ray. "Focus on Women at ATA Meeting." Toronto: *Globe and Mail,* 5 August 1985: S13.

Hofsess, John. "Pollock is an exception to rule." *The Albertan's Sunday Tab ,* 7 January 1979: T03.

Nunn, Robert C. "Performing Fact: Canadian Documentary Theatre." *Canadian Literature,* 103 (Winter 1984): 55-56.

Nunn, Robert C. "Sharon Pollock's Plays: A Review Article." *Theatre History in Canada,* 5.1 (Spring 1984): 72-83.

Page, Malcom. "Sharon Pollock: Committed Playwright." *Canadian Drama/L'Art dramatique canadien,* 5.2 (Fall 1979): 104-11.

Pollock, Sharon. "Comment from the Playwright." Program from *Vancouver: The Playhouse Theatre Centre* of BC, New Company, Festival Habitat, 17-22 May 1976.

Pollock, Sharon. "Blood Relations." *Plays by Women, Volume Three,* ed. Michelene Wandor. London: Methuen, 1984.

Pollock, Sharon. *Blood Relations and Other Plays.* Edmonton: NeWest Press, 1981.

Pollock, Sharon. *The Komagata Maru Incident*. Toronto: Playwrights Co-op, 1978.

Pollock, Sharon. *Out Goes You*. Unpublished.

Pollock, Sharon. *Doc*. Toronto: Playwrights Canada, 1984.

Pollock, Sharon. "Generations." *Blood Relations and Other Plays*. Edmonton: NeWest Press, 1981.

Pollock, Sharon. *Walsh*. Vancouver: Talonbooks, 1973; revised, 1974; revised, 1983.

Pollock, Sharon. "Whiskey Six Cadenza." *NeWest Plays by Women*. Edmonton: NeWest Press, 1987.

Wallace, Robert, and Cynthia Zimmerman. *The Work: Conversations with English-Canadian Playwrights*. Toronto: Coach House, 1982.

Wandor, Michelene. *Plays by Women, Volume Two*. London: Methuen, 1983.

Wilson, Ann. "The Politics of the Script." *Canadian Theatre Review*, 43 (Summer 1985): 174-79.

Wyman, Max. "Komagata Maru: The clash of symbols." *The Vancouver Sun*, 21 January 1976: 43.

Feminism and Metadrama

Role-playing in Blood Relations

Susan Stratton

In her introduction to a new collection of feminist essays on contemporary women's theatre, Lynda Hart reminds us of Marilyn Frye's analogy between women and stagehands.[1] In the foreground of our collective world view, Frye observes, is "Phallocratic Reality," constructed by men and presented as objective reality. The analogue is dramatic realism, which depends on sustaining the onstage illusion of reality. In both cases, attention is not to stray to the background. Women's experience in the one instance and offstage reality in the other are kept in the dark, while men's experience and onstage action are illuminated. Feminism moves our focus of attention to the background, as does theatre that challenges the conventions of realism (Frye 170). Hart speaks of "a shift in the last decade" of feminist criticism "towards rigorous exploration of the language of representation itself" (Hart 2).The dramatic analogue would be metadrama, those plays about drama and theatre that examine the conventions – the language – of dramatic representation itself.

Feminism and metadrama intersect in the role-playing of Sharon Pollock's *Blood Relations*. The character of Lizzie Borden is created at the point of intersection. Her character is defined both by the social role-playing that was imposed on her by family and the rest of society in 1892 and by the Actress's 1902 performance as Lizzie, when she imaginatively creates Lizzie's part in the ax murders. The first kind of role-playing is a feminist concern; the second is metadramatic.

The part of the play that recreates the events of 1892 presents the independent, strong-minded Lizzie in contrast with her mousy older sister Emma. Except that she is not married, Emma is what society, represented by the senior Bordens, expects of a woman. "Emma's a good girl," as her father says (35). Lizzie rebels against the role she is expected to play. She struggles against the role of the dutiful daughter, alternately pleading with and raging at her father. She is contemptuous of the expectation that she will pose as eligible and alluring when she has no wish to become a dutiful wife and mother. Her flirtation with the married Catholic doctor is carried on out of boredom and defiance, not because she is attracted to him, as her father assumes, but because she can amuse herself and annoy her family without running the risk of being pushed into marriage with him. Lizzie's hatred of dependence and her individuality cannot be accommodated in her society. Her father, whom she loves, approves of her only when she wears a mask that horrifies her, when she pretends things she doesn't feel, when she reflects her father's idea of femininity.

The first act closes on a highly theatrical depiction of Mr. Borden's slaughter of Lizzie's birds. Act II opens on the subject of death, not directly Lizzie's reflections on her father's destruction of the birds she loved, but her memory of her father drowning a puppy during one of her childhood stays at the family farm. The puppy was "different," Lizzie reflects – as she is "different" – and "different" things are killed. The atmosphere of death is pervasive from this point on.

Mr. Borden's destruction of Lizzie's birds recalls Jean's destruction of Julie's bird in *Miss Julie*. Pollock keeps the outcome of Strindberg's play before us, as Lizzie considers the possibility of taking her own life. The trap tightens around Lizzie, as her prospects for further freedom are cut off by the transfer of her father's property to her stepmother. As death looms ever larger, the only options are Julie's – suicide – or murder. "I want to die, but something inside won't let me," Lizzie says. "Something inside says no" (54). So the murders can be seen as an act of strength, an assertion of Lizzie's own value, of the repressed woman's right to life.

Lizzie's parents portray traditional modes of thought. Mrs. Borden, whom Lizzie despises, is caught in the same trap as Lizzie, but she accepts it as inevitable. Mr. Borden is driven frantic by his inability to make his daughter conform to the only role for women he understands. He is bewildered and frustrated by her refusal to accept what he is convinced is best for her. Lizzie's murder of the senior Bordens can be taken as an attempt to destroy blind male authority and female acceptance of it.

In the part of *Blood Relations* that depicts events that take place in the Borden household in 1892, then, we are shown a woman who rebels against the social role expected of women; the role is so far from her sense of her true identity that she feels herself being destroyed by it; the role is a killer, and she reacts by becoming a murderer, enacting instead of suffering destruction. This fits Helene Keyssar's emphasis in *Feminist Theatre* on transformation rather than recognition as characteristic of feminist theatre. From the time of Aristotle, Keyssar observes, the recognition scene has been central to drama, but feminist drama presents metamorphosis in place of self-discovery (xiv). Lizzie Borden's transformation from repressed daughter to murderer, from victim of society to destroyer of paternal authority, is an instance of such transformation. The key development of the play is not a moment of self-recognition but rather Lizzie's decision to change, to seize power and strike out for freedom after a lifetime of powerlessness in which every possibility for freedom has been denied her.

Pollock's feminist exploration of social roles and their limitations is complex in a number of ways I do not propose to discuss in detail. Lizzie's Lesbian relationship with the Actress[3] accounts for her rebellion against traditional courtship; her homosexuality is just one of the ways in which her individuality runs counter to the prescribed social role that stifles her. The contrast between Mrs. Borden, who is able to use the woman's role to her advantage, and her stepdaughters, who cannot, is instructive. And certainly it is noteworthy that it is the very strength of society's conviction that woman must be what popular belief dictates she is that acquits Lizzie in the murder trial. The Defense moves towards his concluding assertion of Lizzie's innocence with: "Gentlemen! If this gentlewoman is capable of such an act – I say to you – look to your daughters – if this gentlewoman is capable of such an act, which of us can lie abed at night, hear a step upon the stairs, a rustle in the hall, a creak outside the door...?" (36)

Blood Relations is a feminist play, but it goes beyond the feminist study of the restrictions of women's social roles and the feminist emphasis on the possibility for change. These ingredients were in the early version of the play called *My Name Is Lisbeth*, performed at Douglas College in 1976, a version that was judged wanting by Pollock and by others.[4] The play that earned the first Governor General's Award for drama and many productions across Canada and beyond is more – not only a feminist study of social roles but a sophisticated metadramatic exploration of role playing. The University of Calgary's collection of Sharon Pollock's manuscripts[5] shows how she worked to create and strengthen the metadramatic impact of her play. In *My Name Is Lisbeth*, there is no Actress, no 1902 frame, just the depiction of the events of 1892 in the Borden household. Later, the Actress and the role-playing device are introduced. Still later, the Actress's role is strengthened to the point at which it dominates the play. Even after she published the script in 1981, Pollock extended its metadramatic suggestions further in a production she directed.

In *Blood Relations*, Lizzie's choice of murder in response to the threat of self-destruction is portrayed by the Actress in 1902; we do not see a "direct" presentation of the events or characters of 1892, but rather what Pollock calls "a dream thesis" (13) – all the characters of 1892 are imaginary. Miss Lizzie (the script's designation for the 1902 character), who has been tried and acquitted, will not say whether or not she committed the murders. The Actress comments on Miss Lizzie's awareness of the "fascination in the ambiguity . . . If you didn't I should be disappointed . . . and if you did I should be horrified" (20). If she didn't, Miss Lizzie is nothing more than "a pretentious small-town spinster," and the Actress is doubtful whether that is better than being a murderer (21). Certainly the ambiguity was central to Pollock's conception, which is reminiscent of Pirandello's *Right You Are (If You Think So)* and *Henry IV*. In a holograph note on the back of the penultimate page of a nearly final version of *Blood Relations*, Pollock wrote, "The ambiguity of her art is what keeps the Lizzie Borden legend alive" (*MS* 54.5.3). Historically, the ambiguity is maintained by the fact that, although Lizzie was acquitted, no one else was ever convicted of the murders. In the play, Miss Lizzie's relationship with the Actress apparently depends on the fascination of that ambiguity. Metadramatically, the central ambiguity of the play is the relationship between Miss Lizzie and the Actress – not the sexual relationship, but their identities and their interaction in creating the events of 1892.

The device of the Actress's creation, under Miss Lizzie's guidance, of the circumstances that lead up to the murders, and then a gradual move into her part in such a way that the enactment of the murders is her own creation, produces the desired ambiguity. It also extends the exploration of role-playing with a construct that is overtly metadramatic. Like feminism which rejects conventional social roles, metadrama subverts dramatic conventions by calling attention to them, spotlighting the assumptions about the relationship between drama and life that underlie most dramatic performance. We have traditionally thought in terms of difference: actors play roles on stage, while offstage they revert to their true selves. Drama is about life, even if a play inevitably presents a perception of life rather than an imitation of life, as Richard Hornby argues in *Drama, Metadrama and Perception*. Metadrama is about our means of perception, about how we organize our experiences to present them in dramatic form; "it occurs whenever the subject of a play turns out to be, in some sense, drama itself" (31). Much feminist drama, including *Blood Relations*, is about socially dictated gender roles. But *Blood Relations* is also about how we perceive role-playing itself. There is considerable use in the play of dreams, game-playing, images, all of which point to perception, rather than action, as central to the play. Most evident of all in this complex of non-naturalistic devices is the central device of role-playing, which raises questions of identity and reminds us "that all human roles are relative, that identities are learned rather than innate" (Hornby 72).

In the early stages of the Actress's adoption of Lizzie's role, she is tentative, guided by Miss Lizzie in her role of the maid Bridget to understand the family relationships and the situation. Miss Lizzie/Bridget subtly corrects her mistakes and leads her towards an understanding of her role. As the Actress gains confidence in her role, Miss Lizzie, as Bridget, fades into the background. The Actress is never assigned a name of her own. She blends into Lizzie, both on stage as they change roles and in Pollock's designations in the script, where she is first the Actress, then Lizzie and sometimes Actress/Lizzie. Even before the role-playing is undertaken, Miss Lizzie has a line which begins to blur the line drawn between the two: "You look like me, or how I think I look, or how I ought to look . . . , sometimes you think like me . . . do you feel that?" The Actress concurs: "Sometimes" (19). The two can be seen to comprise one complete identity, each supplying something that is lacking in the other.

By Act II, the Actress is fully in control of her portrayal. Her Lizzie is now an independent creation, though we may not realize it as the drama unfolds. There are many reminders that Miss Lizzie and the Actress are role-playing in Act I, but there are fewer in Act II. The outlines of Lizzie's character are consistent with those developed under Miss Lizzie's guidance in Act I, but the Actress's performance of Lizzie's actions on the day of the murders is almost completely uninfluenced by Miss Lizzie/Bridget, who is mostly absent from the stage during the buildup to the first murder. Bridget exits just after the beginning of Act II, reappears twice, briefly, instructing the Actress/Lizzie only once – "You mustn't cry" – before the Actress/Lizzie leads Mrs. Borden upstairs to her death.

Later, Miss Lizzie/Bridget appears unobtrusively just before the Actress/Lizzie picks up the ax to murder her father as he sleeps. Under Pollock's direction, the blackout that occurs just as the ax hesitates at the apex of its path was accompanied by a chilling scream. Who screams? One thinks of Bridget, horrified by Lizzie's deed. But could it be that Lizzie is horrified by the Actress's depiction of her as murderer of the father she loved? (Of course it could have been pure theatricality – just a scream, to underscore the horror of the moment.

Because the Actress's portrayal of Lizzie as an ax murderer is so vivid and so psychologically convincing, and because our absorption in the unfolding events of Act II is virtually undisturbed by reminders that this Lizzie is an actress's creation – despite the theatricality of the blackout at the moment before the "onstage" murder – an audience is very likely to accept the truth of events as they have been portrayed.[8] However, the end of the play provokes second thoughts on both the truth of the events just witnessed and the characterization of Lizzie as feminist heroine.

The characterization of Lizzie as a strong and independent woman in 1892 is undercut by the realization that in the frame play ten years later, Miss Lizzie still lives in the same house (which she had earlier longed to escape) and she still lives with her conventional sister Emma. Her dream of social prominence in a corner house on the hill remains unrealized, as does her alternate wish to live by herself on the family farm. Emma's concern about what people will think still intrudes on Miss Lizzie's life. Miss Lizzie has formed a bond with the unconventional Actress, but she is still chained to the old values, represented by Emma. Quite realistically, she has been unable to free herself entirely from the social role she might have hoped to escape with the death of the older Bordens — her transformation is limited. She is independent enough to maintain a socially unacceptable liaison with the Actress, but hardly more independent than she was ten years earlier in her flirtation with the married doctor. Lizzie occupies a middle ground between Emma and the Actress on the scale ranging from social constraint to freedom from social role-playing. It is the Actress, the *professional* role player, who is freely unconventional, uninhibited, strong. And, as the last line of the play (Miss Lizzie's "I didn't. You did.") reminds us, it is the Actress who enacted the murders, who might be said to have created a Lizzie strong enough to commit them.

In the final scene, Lizzie rebuffs Emma's persistent questioning about whether she committed the murders. In a sequence which Pollock originally placed early in the play but which gained power when she moved it to the end, Lizzie turns the spotlight on Emma: "Did you never stop and think that if I did, then you were guilty too? It was you brought me up . . . Did you ever stop and think that I was like a puppet, your puppet . . . me saying all the things you felt like saying, me doing all the things you felt like doing, me spewing forth, me hitting out. . . ." (70). This speech suggests a parallel between the Actress's creation of Lizzie and Emma's creation of Lizzie, an assertion of psychological reality in which the differences between life and art fade into insignificance. And the implication that Lizzie is what Emma created is no more true or false than that she is what the Actress created. The Actress projects herself into a situation described by Lizzie and creates a Lizzie who murders her parents. Emma, Lizzie claims, created Lizzie to respond to a situation as Emma never dared to herself — as the Actress would respond. The good girl needs the feminist, which is why

Emma stays with Lizzie, even though she has good reason to fear her. One might say that Emma deliberately absented herself from the home on the day of the murders, to give Lizzie more opportunity to act. A feminist reading would see how all three women share complicity in the murder – and the stage direction has the Actress looking at the audience when Lizzie concludes the play with "You did," which suggests an extension of complicity to the audience as well.

However, Lizzie is not necessarily either Emma's creation or the Actress's. She is ultimately an unknown. As Lizzie claims in trying to explain to her father that she cannot live simply as the reflection of what others want to see, "If no one looks in the mirror, I'm not even there, I don't exist!" (39). Both Emma and the Actress as creators constitute a defense for Miss Lizzie, barriers to any claim she might make to autonomy, to self-definition – or to responsibility. But this recognition, interesting as it may be to us intellectually, carries relatively little dramatic impact. Dramatically, the truth is that "Lizzie" is a murderer. The murders are psychologically convincing, theatrically vivid. They are not realistically presented – the "onstage" murder is highly stylized, in fact, not actually depicted at all. But the drama is more powerfully convincing than the theoretical possibility of a different reality. The drama satisfies, leaving an audience incurious about the reality, despite the invitation in the play's conclusion to dismiss the staged events as just an imaginative construct of the Actress's. Lizzie's life remains an enigma, but the Actress's dramatic portrayal is vivid and arresting. The Actress outshines her subject, and the drama eclipses whatever the reality might have been. The art is more real than life.

Role-playing may be destructive when the role is dictated by social expectations, but the nameless Actress, the professional role-player, is the most vitally alive, most independent, individual character in *Blood Relations.* Her creation of Lizzie is equally alive, and the reality she creates is the one we are most likely to believe. In the process of developing this compelling creation, Pollock asks some important questions about role-playing. How do we distinguish between a role and the self? Has the self in fact any reality apart from the role? Are we simply exchanging one role for another if we reject the first? If Lizzie is not just a small-town spinster, the role defined for her by society, then is she a murderess? That role, it turns out, is defined by the Actress, or in another sense, perhaps by Emma, unconsciously creating a puppet to do what she dares not do herself.

Lizzie refuses definition by society when she feels like it; she hands Emma the responsibility for having defined her when it suits her to do so, and she declines to accept the Actress's definition of her after encouraging her to create such a definition. In so doing, Lizzie disappears into non-entity, supplanted in our minds by the stronger reality of the Actress who creates a role and lives it without ambiguity. In *Blood Relations,* then, there is not only feminist rejection of a social role, but philosophical acknowledgement of the fact that role-playing is essential to existence. This brings us to questions about how and by whom these roles are defined and about whether we can ever really be known apart from them. Feminists, who reject traditional social roles for women and who may blame men for creating the roles they find themselves playing, are now facing the challenge of the difficult questions raised in Pollock's metadramatic exploration of role playing.

NOTES

1 This article is a revised version of a paper given at the ACTH/AHTC Annual Conference held at Laval University, 1989. It was originally published under the name Susan Stone-Blackburn in *Modern Drama*.

2 Robert C. Nunn offers an interesting view of the key to the play as a dual recognition, suggesting that the last line of the play would cause the Actress to recognize that she too is capable of murdering for freedom and that Lizzie's speech a few lines earlier about being Emma's puppet shows a realization that she has not acted freely after all: "Two protagonists, two recognitions, crossing each other" ("Sharon Pollock's Plays." *Theatre History in Canada*, 5.1 [Spring 1984]: 79). Though I do not disagree with the essence of his reading, I will argue that Pollock's emphasis is otherwise. In particular, it would seem odd for Pollock to express a key self-recognition as an unanswered accusation by another character in the last line of the play.

3 In an interview with Robert Wallace, Pollock says that, though her research turned up many references to Lizzie Borden's friendship with actress Nance O'Neill, none of her sources hints at a homosexual relationship. Pollock finds this unremarkable, given the dates and backgrounds of her sources. See Robert Wallace and Cynthia Zimmerman. *The Work*. Toronto: The Coach House Press, 1982: 124.

4 Malcolm Page, in a discussion of this early version, concludes that "*My Name Is Lisbeth* comes out as a thin and tentative look at Victorian middle-class family life, by *The Heiress* of *The Barretts of Wimpole Street*... No clear view of Lizzie, no reason for writing, comes through." (Malcolm Page. "Sharon Pollock: Committed Playwright." *Canadian Drama* 5.2 [Fall 1979]: 109-110.)

5 An inventory of the manuscript collection in the University of Calgary Library's Special Collections has been published: Apollonia Steele and Jean Tener, eds. *The Sharon Pollock Papers, First Accession*. Calgary: University of Calgary Press, 1989.

6 The script opens with the Actress in Lizzie's parlour rehearsing lines. This opening establishes her as an actress, and her speech, Hermione's reflections on her difficulty in defending herself against Leontes' accusation in Act III of *The*

Winter's Tale, points toward the subject of Lizzie's guilt or innocence. In the 1988 production by Theatre 80 in Calgary, Pollock modified the opening substantially with very minor alterations to the dialogue. She had the Actress dash breathlessly into Miss Lizzie's parlour from outside and address Hermione's lines to the offstage Miss Lizzie, whom the Actress knows will be jealously wondering why her lover is late. Thus, even the opening speech functions metadramically, as the Actress's stage world and " real " world combine.

7   According to Michele Merrill, the stage manager for Theatre 1980s production, the scream was taped and was probably Pollock's own since she did a lot of work on the sound.

8   Most commentators on the play think Lizzie's guilt is not really in doubt, though of course they recognize the ambiguity. A reasonable cross-section can be found in L.W. Conolly. "Modern Canadian Drama: Some Critical Perspectives." *Canadian Drama*, 11:1 (Spring 1985): 188-195.

WORKS CITED

Frye, Marilyn. *The Politics of Reality: Essays in Feminist Theory*. New York: The Crossing Press, 1983.

Hart, Lynda, ed. *Making a Spectacle: Feminist Essays on Contemporary Women's Theatre*. Ann Arbor: University of Michigan Press, 1989.

Hornby, Richard. *Drama, Metadrama and Perception*. Lewisburg: Bucknell University Press, 1986.

Keyssar, Helene. *Feminist Theatre*. London: Macmillan, 1984.

Pollock, Sharon. *Blood Relations and Other Plays*. Edmonton: Ne-West Press, 1981.

Steele, Apollonia, and Jean Tener, eds. *The Sharon Pollock Papers, First Accession*. Calgary: University of Calgary Press, 1989.

Crossing Borders

Sharon Pollock's Revisitation of Canadian Frontiers

Anne F. Nothof

Sharon Pollock's "history plays" are essentially iconoclastic, deconstructing comfortable assumptions about the growth of the Canadian nation through the gradual and peaceful integration of "others" from across the borders. In two of her early plays – *Walsh*, which premiered at Theatre Calgary in 1973, and *The Komagata Maru Incident*, which was first produced at the Vancouver Playhouse in 1976 – she demonstrates how the politics of exclusion determined the characteristics of a "white man's country." In *Fair Liberty's Call*,[1] which opened at the Patterson Theatre in Stratford, Ontario in July 1993, she deconstructs the "Loyalist myth" which assumes that Canada's democratic freedoms owe a great deal to the courageous, independent exiles from America, who crossed the border to begin a more egalitarian society. The title of Pollock's play is shown, in fact, to be ironic: there is little difference between the policy or actions of rebel and loyalist, Patriot and Tory. The contentious issues which fuelled the War of Independence are replicated in Canada. In all three plays, borders are imposed – between countries, between individuals – in the interests of securing or protecting property. Political or ethical principles are modified to serve basically acquisitive impulses, and government policy expresses the entrenched bigotry and greed of an established population, all immigrants or the descendants of immigrants. In an introductory note to the published version of *The Komagata Maru Incident* (1978), Sharon Pollock demonstrates the importance of a revisionist view of Canadian history: "As a Canadian, I feel that much of our history has been mis-represented and even hidden from us. Until we recognize our past, we cannot change our future." "History" is a mythology, a narrative constructed by those in power to sustain and justify their power. More recently, however, historiography has engaged in a de-mythologizing process, revisiting the past in an attempt to ascertain cultural ideology:

> Historiographers and literary theorists in recent years have concerned themselves with the writing of history less as the uncovering of an objective body of material actually existing in the past than as the invention of a narrative that exists as a function of the society and culture that produces it in the present. Post-modern historiography recognizes that the past, insofar as it is external and objective, can only exist as fragments, "facts" and documents that are in their own cultural terms, impenetrable. Historiography, then, becomes the ongoing process of remaking history, of "making it new," as fiction and myth. (Knowles 228)

Sharon Pollock's plays are less concerned with history as a "record of past activity" than with the "intellectual climate in which it was composed" (Berger ix), insidious assumptions and attitudes which may still effect public and private policy – "upholding compromise over compassion, legality over justice" (Pollock, quoted in Hutchinson S5). They reflect a "progressive" view of history, which is "cynical about ideas, theories and ideologies" (Berger 62) that may be convenient camouflage or rationalization. One of these ideologies is that of Canada's growth as a democratic nation, freely welcoming immigrants from around the world across its borders, and balancing conflicting regional, racial, and economic pressures, in contrast to the violent revolutions and wars bred by intolerance in the United States. In *Walsh*, *The Komagata Maru Incident*, and *Fair Liberty's Call*, Pollock shatters this myth of Canadian moral superiority: there is little difference between the public and private policy of the two countries. As Canadian historian, Frank Underhill, has maintained, in many ways the United States is simply Canada writ large.

Moreover, Sharon Pollock shows that public policy is predicated on, and effected through individual choices: although her protagonists are subject to large historical or political forces, they still have a degree of freedom of choice – whether to compromise justice, whether to subvert compassion. Borders may be psychological and philosophical as well as political. In each play, choices are made as to which side of the border to occupy or defend, and whether it is possible to cross borders with integrity. Pollock believes that her preoccupation with conflict between personal integrity and political expediency is a very Canadian phenomenon, conditioned by geographic, economic, and political factors:

> All of my plays deal with the same concern. I think I write the same play over and over again. It's a play about an individual who is directed to or compelled to follow a course of action of which he or she begins to examine the morality. Circumstances force a decision, usually the authority (family, society, government) is removed emotionally or geographically from the protagonist, and it usually doesn't end very well. It doesn't resolve in happiness. I think that is a very Canadian

thing, actually, that comes from living in Alberta or the Maritimes and feeling that Ottawa never seems to understand what it is that is required in these places (Pollock, in Much 210).

In both *Walsh* and *The Komagata Maru Incident*, the borders are rigidly maintained, and justice is compromised through the imposition of devious legalities. The protagonists deny important aspects of themselves in conforming to a central government authority which understands nothing of the personal consequences of its decisions to those attempting to cross the border, or to those obliged to defend it. *Walsh* dramatizes the consequences of the Hunkpapa Sioux's retreat across the Canadian border after the Custer debacle in 1874 at Little Bighorn. Although Pollock takes some liberties with historical detail in illuminating the salient issues, the consequences of Canadian government policy towards the Sioux in the North West Territories are the same in fact as in fiction: virtual genocide. Whereas the American government had used weapons and warfare to exterminate the Sioux, the Canadian government used starvation, as the choric character, Harry, the wagonmaster, points out in *Walsh*:

> Sir John A's policy for dealin with the Sioux was an all round winner – beats Custer all to hell. Not half so messy as ridin' into tube-like hollows at ungodly hours of the mornin' – and no need for a marchin' band. Quiet, simple and effective. Do not delay in returning to the United States, for that course is the only alternative to death by starvation. So Sittin' Bull left the Canadian West (112).

Pressured by the American government to force the return of the Sioux, Sir John A. Macdonald initially compromised by decreeing that the Sioux could remain only as long as they were self-sufficient: "The Queen won't feed or clothe [them] as she does her own Indians" (49). The Sioux are regarded as property, to be dispensed with as is politically expedient. Yet, as Chief Gall points out to Major Walsh, the individual charged with effecting government policy in the Territories, the Sioux nation was promised protection by the British when they fought against the rebels in the American Revolution, and he carries a George III medal as proof of the promise (40). In fact, the Indians who supported the British in the Revolution and the War of 1812 could be considered "Loyalists," as historian Wallace Brown points out:

> In 1876 the remarks of Sitting Bull to Inspector J. M. Walsh, when the Sioux chief brought his people to Canada after the defeat of Custer at Little Big Horn, suggest that the Sioux considered that they had always had a loyalist option. Sitting Bull told Walsh that they were originally Shaganosh (British) and that during the War of 1812 they had been told by a representative of their Shaganosh father (George III) that they could move into British territory if they found things difficult in the United States (203).

In *Walsh* the Sioux do not acknowledge the imposition of borders, nor that they are the "property" of one government or another. The sacred circle encompasses all, as Sitting Bull explains: "All of the universe is enclosed and revealed in the sacred circle" (61). Sitting Bull attempts to preserve the integrity of the Hunkpapa Sioux in the Territories as wholly self-sufficient, living in peace as hunters. But the buffalo are disappearing on the prairies, and the Americans fire the border to keep the remaining animals for "their own" Indians, as well as to starve the Sioux in Canada into submission, and to force the Canadian government into making a decision to return the Sioux for American "justice."

In *Walsh*, the policies of the Canadian government are conveyed through the "messenger," Colonel MacLeod, to Major Walsh: "The Sioux have no future here in Canada" (84). To Walsh's argument that the Hunkpapa Sioux have as much right to stay in the North West Territories as the Santee Sioux had in Manitoba, MacLeod responds that "Out here [Walsh doesn't] see the whole picture. There are other considerations" (85). Sitting Bull and his people are used as "pawns," sacrificed for political expediency, and the Prime Minister orders that they be no longer provided with food, clothing, or ammunition. Charged with effecting government decisions, Major Walsh struggles with his own sense of justice, and his compassion and admiration for Sitting Bull and his people, but faced with the ruination of his career if he fails to comply, he opts for "self-preservation," man's strongest instinct. The Sioux are escorted across the border, where Sitting Bull is arrested and sent to Fort Randall. However, Pollock also shows the psychological damage which Major Walsh suffers as a consequence of compromising his principles.

The consequences of imposing borders – psychological and political – are witnessed by the new recruit, Clarence, who has come west with the North West Mounted Police to realize the frontier myth of "freedom" and "manifest destiny":

> out here in the territories, that was where everything was happen', the Indian Wars, the Openin' of the West, and Wild Bill Hickock sittin' on the biggest, blackest horse you ever saw (72).

As expounded by American historian Frederick Jackson Turner, the concept of the "frontier" was identified with "the hither edge of free land," "the meeting ground between savagery and civilization," "that zone of settlement nearest the wilderness, wherein society and government are loosely or incompletely organized" (Berger 118). Clarence learns that this myth is a lie, and that "civilization" and "savagery" may be closely allied. He believes that no people should be starved into submission: "just cause you wish they'd move someplace else, you don't let people starve! You can't do things like that"(75).

Starvation as a political tactic to keep undesirables out of the country is used again in 1914, with the incident of the Komagata Maru, a Japanese freighter carrying 376 potential immigrants from the Punjab in India to Vancouver. Sharon Pollock's dramatization of the events is a freely rendered "theatrical impression of an historical event seen through the optique of the stage and the mind of the playwright" (Playwright's Note), but the issues are compellingly clear: a racist government policy reflects the pervasive public opinion that Canada remain a "white man's country." *The Komagata Maru Incident*, first produced in Vancouver in 1976, may also have been inspired by the publication in 1975 of Ted Ferguson's *A White Man's Country: An Exercise in Canadian Prejudice*. Ferguson provides a detailed account of the standoff between immigration official, Inspector Malcolm Reid, and Gurdit Singh, who organized the voyage, and shows the complicated ramifications in the Vancouver Sikh community and in India. Moreover anti-Sikh demonstrations took place in Vancouver in the early 1970s. For Sharon Pollock, history is never safely confined to the past. It must constantly be scrutinized for the lies it perpetuates and the truths it may subvert, as she explains in a programme note for the first production of the play:

> To know where we are going, we must know where we have been and what we have come from. Our attitude towards the non-white peoples of the world and of Canada is one that suffers from the residue effects of centuries of oppressive policies which were given moral and ethical credence by the fable of racial superiority ... The attitudes expressed by the general populace of that time, and paraphrased throughout the play, are still around today, and until we face this fact, we can never change it.

As Pollock outlines in her Note to the published text of the play, "By the early 1900s the Canadian government believed it had devised an airtight method to virtually exclude immigration from Asia" by passing two bills which did not appear to discriminate against East Indians, but which in fact made immigration from India almost impossible: the first imposed a "head" tax of $200 which few could afford; the second prohibited the landing of any immigrant who came other than by continuous passage. Ironically, as Chief Justice Gordon Hunter ruled, every citizen of India was a British subject, and could go anywhere he pleased in the Empire (Ferguson 7). However, Immigration officials, acting on government policies, denied the Sikh immigrants landing rights, and for seven weeks they awaited their fate, denied food and water until they agreed to return to India. The night the ship arrived in the harbour, Sir Richard McBride, the premier of British Columbia, stated: "To admit Orientals in large numbers would mean in the end the extinction of the white people, and we always have in mind the necessity of keeping this a white man's country" (Ferguson 10). H. H. Stevens, the West Coast Member of Parliament, who kept an eye on the Komagata Maru situation for Prime Minister Borden, was also a fervent exponent of non-white exclusion, as he made clear in a February 1912 edition of the *Monetary Times*:

> The Hindus will not assimilate but they will segregate in ill-ventilated and unsanitary surroundings, harbouring disease and immorality. Their word is unreliable and this is so far established that many of our judges will not take their cases unsupported by white men (Ferguson 50).

The mayor of Vancouver, T.S. Baxter, refused to send food to the Komagata Maru, and the standoff between officials and Sikhs became a public spectacle which attracted crowds to Vancouver harbour. Pollock develops this image of a public entertainment or circus[2] through the structure of her play: the narrator functions as a ring-master, introducing the players and the acts. He is also the voice of public policy and public opinion – and is appropriately named T.S. The Sikhs are represented in the person of an Indian woman. Although there were only three women on board the Komagata Maru, and all were allowed on shore, Pollock's representative of the excluded group is doubly marginalized – by race and by gender. This play is not only about political borders.

As the agent of political policy, Pollock casts a minor character in the actual events, a "borderline" Canadian of mixed parents – his father being a British sergeant stationed in northern India, and his mother a woman from the Punjab. Inspector William Hopkinson's family history is accurately replicated in Pollock's play, as it provides an ironic insight into the nature of bigotry in Canada – that in a land of immigrants there is little tolerance for newcomers, who become convenient scapegoats for social problems. Hopkinson has established a network of informers in the Sikh community, to determine whether any are illegal immigrants or possible seditionists conspiring against British authority in India, many of whom were slipping across the Canada-U.S. border. *The Komagata Maru Incident* focuses primarily on the issue of "illegal immigration," however, and does not explore the revolutionary activities of the Ghadr, or its connections with the Germans in securing arms just before the outbreak of the First World War. The role of the German character in the play, Georg Braun, serves to comment on the Arian-supremacy philosophy implicit in government policy and explicit in the attitudes of racist Canadians, and on the fascist techniques employed by immigration officials in disposing of "undesirables." As Georg cynically observes:

> My friends tell me they [the government] have promised them everything and will give them nothing. That's called diplomacy, eh Bill? (41)

Hopkinson is initially a wholly unsympathetic character, with overtly racist ideas and motivated primarily by career considerations, as he admits to the prostitute, Evy:

> HOPKINSON. One has to make decisions. Commitments to one side or another.
> EVY. What side are you on?
> HOPKINSON. The winning side.
> EVY. Are you winning? (40)

As his own heritage is gradually exposed by Evy, however, he is forced to acknowledge his self-destructive hypocrisy, and he accepts his death at the hands of the revolutionary Sikh, Mewa Singh, as a just retribution for his lack of compassion for others, and his betrayal of his heritage. In choosing to effect repressive policies, he has denied his own humanity.

Interestingly, Pollock sets *The Komagata Maru Incident* in a brothel – perhaps as an ironic reversal of the perceived "moral" majority values. The two prostitutes in the brothel are also victims of "white *man's*" power, and survive only in terms of white men's rules – the power that money can buy: "No tickee, no laundree," as Sophie points out to Georg, ironically and unconsciously drawing a correspondence between her situation and that of the Chinese in Vancouver. Evy's voice, however, is the voice of compassion in the play. She sees through Hopkinson's self-delusion and recognizes that he is being used by those in power to effect their own personal and political ends – just like the Major in *Walsh*. The imposition of borders may be arbitrary and unjust, and frontiers may be a reification of political and social prejudice.

The frontier in Pollock's most recent "historic" play, *Fair Liberty's Call*, is maritime Canada in 1784 when New Brunswick was established as an autonomous province after a massive influx of 16,000 Loyalists to Nova Scotia from the United States. Although they have crossed a border and are now under British rule, the Loyalists carry the same social and personal baggage which fuelled the American Revolution, and the struggle between independence and authority is replayed. Pollock shows how in one family is enacted the conflicts of the War of Independence, which was more like a civil war than a struggle against external authority, since it took place within each state, and even within families. There were no clearly established borders for the conflict: sons fought against fathers, brothers against brothers, and often individuals or families would change sides to survive. Some subscribed to the ideals of independence, but abhorred the rule of the mob. Inevitably, however, all were forced to choose a side. In *Fair Liberty's Call*, these divided loyalties are evident in the Roberts family: the father, George, whose name ironically alludes to the British monarch, has attempted to survive by playing to both sides – changing his allegiance as the situation warrants, but his loyalty is primarily to his own material interests, and his concern in his new country is for the acquisition of property – the land promised by the British to exiled Loyalists. As he unfurls the British flag in the first scene, he makes clear his version of the story, and reveals his primary concern for property and power, for which he has sacrificed his own children. He is a "buyer and a seller" who will "sell his soul"(22) to get what he wants. Moreover, he assumes that his family "will do whatever is required"(25) to protect his interests.

His eldest son, Richard, has rebelled against these "values" and joined the Patriots. He has served under Benedict Arnold in the seige of Quebec, and then killed in action under the same turncoat at Saratoga. In Pollock's play, the historic ironies multiply, as allegiances are changed and borders crossed. Facts are indeed stranger than fiction, as the elder daughter, Annie, comments:

> Here are the facts – papa was for representation in British parliament; Richard for separation and independence. And they fought, first each other, and then . . . it's true he was taken, held in the Long Island Prison Ships, and then – there was a prisoner exchange and . . . later he died, we were told, in one of the battles they called Saratoga where he fought under Arnold. *(She smiles.)* That's right. Benedict Arnold. That's not fiction, that's fact. *(She laughs.)* Second time cause he served under Arnold at the Seige of Quebec. My Rebel brother served under Benedict Arnold. Isn't that funny? (14)

The second son, Edward, has chosen the side of the British, and joined the Loyalist regiment which was involved in the slaughter of civilians at Cherry Valley. Unable to live with the horror, he shoots himself in his own home. His place is taken by his twin sister, Emily, who assumes the name "Eddie" and a male persona. She has chosen to cross this "gender border" in order to empower herself, eschewing the victim role which is forced on most women, like her mother. She is also aware that in doing so, she protects her father's interests, since one "son" has fought on each side. Eddie is also involved in horrific massacres – at Waxhaws, South Carolina under Lt. Col. Tarleton, when Rebel troops were slaughtered after they surrendered, and at Cowpens, when the tables were turned. From having lived through these experiences, she is fully aware of the cruel ironies: "What we sowed at Waxhaws, we reaped at King's mountain . . . so it ends up fair all around" (41), but she begins to question the reasons for the war when she sees that the injustices against which she fought are being replicated in New Brunswick.

Cycles of bloody reprisals run through the play: everything goes round and round. The boots of a dead Rebel are taken by a Loyalist soldier, and in turn taken by a rebel. One slaughter is used to justify another: blood begets blood – even after the war is over and a new political border established.[3] Pollock ruthlessly dismantles the Loyalist myth of heroes in exile, perpetuated in song and story:

> Not drooping like poor fugitives they came
> In exodus to our Canadian wilds,
> But full of heart and hope, with heads erect
> And fearless eyes, victorious in defeat
>   (Kirby, quoted in Brown n.p.)

Fair Liberty's Call is a post-modern response to a "patriotic" melodrama written by Catherine Nina Merritt (U.E.L.) in 1807, entitled *"When George the Third Was King": An Historical Drama in III Acts*, set in Boston and in a settler's hut in the backwoods of Canada. The Rebels are depicted as ignorant oafs and drunkards, and the Loyalists as paragons of virtue and courage. When threatened by "wild Indians," the matriarch, Elizabeth, unfurls the Union Jack outside their new home, and eulogizes the values of the British Empire – peace, mercy, and justice.[4]

Joan Roberts, the mother in *Fair Liberty's Call*, has been driven mad by the horrors of war – the loss of two of her sons, and of her home. Like Brecht's Mother Courage, she appears in the first scene with the remnants of her family, dragging a cart with their belongings into unknown territory. But she lacks Mother Courage's aggressive acquisitiveness, and doubts that the land to which they have come will ever become their home: her footprints leave no mark on the soil. The play opens with a verbal montage, the voices of three women – the mother and two daughters, Annie, and Emily/Eddie – telling their story and the story of how "the heartbeat of a country [comes] into bein'"(1). As the Rebel antagonist, Major Anderson, observes, the way a story is told depends on the perspective, on who is telling the story. Pollock tells the story through the differing perspectives of the family members, and of their Loyalist acquaintances who are visiting for a reunion of Tarleton's British Legion – Daniel Wilson, a soldier with a limited political awareness but a sense that things tend to come around in the end, and Major Abijah Williams, who is highly politically motivated. Through Williams, Pollock voices the authoritarian beliefs of the establishment, concerned with protecting its interests in the formation of the new province – the preservation of

Empire, "worth and class"(61), and the acquisition of as much property and power as possible, since "land is money" in New Brunswick. He supports the position of the "Family of 55" which is attempting to establish its authority in New Brunswick, replaying the scenario across the border which incited the rebellion they have fled.[5]

Another social injustice is also perpetuated across the border – the enslavement of the Blacks. They have no more rights in New Brunswick than they did in America: if they had been slaves and fought for the British, then they were granted their freedom, but if they had been Loyalist slaves, then they remained so. Three thousand "free" Blacks emigrated to Nova Scotia, but racial borders were immediately established: they were segregated in the settlement of Birchtown, six miles outside of prosperous Shelburne, and expected to work in subservient jobs as labourers and servants. In *Fair Liberty's Call*, Wullie, who has fought with Eddie in Tarleton's Rangers, is denied his freedom and his land allotment, and scapegoated for murder by Major Williams.

Wullie is supported and Abijah Williams is opposed by the "rebellious" Loyalist Eddie, who believes that the democratic rights for which she has fought in America should now prevail in her new country. Each individual should "exercise freedom of choice" or be "a party to [his] own oppression" (19). Like *Walsh* and *The Komagata Maru Incident*, *Fair Liberty's Call* shows that history is very much a matter of individual choices.

Ironically, each Loyalist is forced into making a decision based on his or her personal and political values by a Rebel soldier, John Anderson, who has crossed the border seeking "justice" for the butchering of his fourteen-year-old brother at Waxhaws. If they do not decide which one is accountable, he will shoot Annie. By recounting her own story of compromised loyalty, the betrayal of a Rebel soldier she had loved to the British, Annie persuades Anderson that justice can never be effected through revenge, and that compassion is the only way to end the cycle of bloody reprisals.[6] She believes that the best way to serve our brothers is to build a better world for our children.

Finally, after Anderson's sudden and mysterious departure, the mother is able to see her footprints in the "virgin" soil, and begins to believe that a new home is possible.[7] There is also the suggestion of harmonious integration with the indigenous native peoples, as Joan tells how an Indian woman has offered her a bowl of earth which she takes into her hands and swallows. This native woman is first evoked by Joan at the beginning of play, accompanied by bird sounds, but her role remains ambiguous, and decidedly unhistorical, since the Micmacs and Malecites were dispossessed with the arrival of the Loyalists. There was no harmonious integration. Racial and social borders were imposed as the Loyalists acquired property and power.[8]

Fair Liberty's Call provides an ironic, revisionist perspective on the history of the Loyalists in New Brunswick. Sharon Pollock skilfully evokes the complexities of the social and ethical issues, the mixed motives, and the political machinations. As with *Walsh* and *The Komagata Maru Incident*, historical "facts" are dramatized freely to raise questions, to interrogate preconceptions and biases. She wants to provoke her audience to a re-examination of their own perspectives on Canada's history, "to come away having been touched by the theatre incident so that the next time they read the paper, it isn't just the headlines (Pollock, quoted in Wallace and Zimmerman 122). Her historiography is subversive and iconoclastic.

For Pollock . . . the "facts" . . . are less important than the imaginative truth, the past that we must allow ourselves to imagine and therefore to bring into being as part of our present. We are, for Pollock, both nationally and individually . . . responsible for what we are and for what we have become. It is incumbent upon us to rethink our comfortable myths of identity if we are to "re-cognize" ourselves and take responsibility for our future (Knowles 240).

NOTES

1. *Fair Liberty's Call* was published by Coach House Press in 1995. For the purposes of this paper, Sharon Pollock kindly made available the prompt script used by the Stage Manager of the Stratford production, Janet Sellery. All quotations are taken from this MS version of the play, with page numbers in parenthesis.
2. In fact, an international circus did come to Vancouver at the time the Komagata Maru was in Burrard Inlet, but the spectacle in the harbour proved to be more popular than the spectacles at the circus. Citizens of Vancouver installed themselves on the roof of Woodward's Department Store, and all along the waterfront when the military was called in to prevent arms being taken to the ship, and especially when the antiquated Canadian destroyer, the Rainbow, was dispatched from Esquimalt to enforce the departure of the Komagata Maru. Parodying Mackenzie King's infamous doublespeak, T.S. in Pollock's play proclaims, "Let our message be – we won't necessarily fire on you – but we will fire on you if necessary" (39).
3. This theme of the endless bloody cycle of reprisals informs another "historic" drama, *Serjeant Musgrave's Dance*, by British playwright, John Arden, which also portrays the consequences of a war fought for "Empire."
4. Elizabeth's speech exemplifies the Loyalist Myth which has informed the more optimistic historical accounts of Canadian history: "Ay! The good old flag doth speak a language of its own that every nation understands; it speaks of peace, of mercy, of justice wrought to suffering men. But, husband, children! What is this I see before me rise? A vision of a

hundred years from now! This little hut hath multiplied a thousand-fold, it is the prototype of buildings made of brick and stone. These trees have changed in aspect, as I look, and some are lofty chimneys, some are spires, and in the streets I see the busy men, a steadfast, loyal, law-abiding race. I see the women, and their little ones, all their faces shine with happy smiles. Within an open space I see a staff, and on it floats the Union Jack. And now the people gather round its base, and there with clasped hands, as if in prayer, they cry with one great voice, "God bless the noble men who sacrificed their wealth, their homes, their friends, their all, to save the good old flag, and plant it safe upon Canadian soil, where underneath its folds, we may enjoy justice and liberty and peace" (Catherine Nina Merritt, *"When George the Third Was King": An Historical Drama in III Acts* [Toronto, 1897], 30).

5   Edward Winslow, for example, attempted to replicate the position of privilege he had enjoyed in America in New Brunswick, which he proposed be made a separate province in order to "manage" the formation of a new community which would provide positions of power for himself and his friends. In 1783, fifty-five Loyalists from New York City petitioned General Guy Carleton for 5000 acres of land each, whereas the standard allotment was for 200 acres per family. They suggested that the new colony would need an elite to lead and organize the masses, and to create a social structure which would ensure order and prosperity. This thinly disguised attempt to establish a social hierarchy was opposed by a group of 600 Loyalists who presented a counter-petition, "denouncing the pretensions of those who had appointed themselves to lead the new society" and refusing "to be tenants to those, most of whom they consider as their superiors in nothing but deeper art and keener policy" (Christopher Moore, *The Loyalists: Revolution, Exile and Settlement* [Toronto, 1984], 144).

6   Annie has much in common with the barmaid, Annie in *Serjeant Musgrave's Dance*, whose indiscriminate compassion for the soldiers contrasts with the rigid imposition of the law by Serjeant Musgrave.

7   Adrienne Rich's view of how "virgin soil" is imprinted by men and women is expressed in "For Julia in Nebraska":
On this beautiful, ever-changing land
– the historical marker says –

man fought to establish a home
(fought whom? the marker is mute.)
They named this Catherland, for Willa Cather,
lesbian – the marker is mute,
the marker white men set on a soil
of broken treaties, Indian blood,
women wiped out in childbirths, massacres –
(*A Wild Patience Has Taken Me This Far: Poems 1978-1981* [New York, 1981], 17)

8   An aborigine haunts the margins of an "historic" play about the first penal colony in Australia, *Our Country's Good*, by Timberlake Wertenbaker, and his role has been variously interpreted in productions as the representative of a people threatened with extinction, the "spirit"of the land, or as a choric respondent to the actions of the white prisoners and officers.

WORKS CITED

Berger, Carl. *The Writing of Canadian History: Aspects of English-Canadian Historical Writing since 1900*, 2nd ed. Toronto: University of Toronto Press, 1986.

Brown, Wallace and Hereward Senior. *Victorious in Defeat: The Loyalists in Canada.* New York: Facts on File Publications, 1984.

Ferguson, Ted. *A White Man's Country: An Exercise in Canadian Prejudice.* Garden City, New York, Doubleday, 1975.

Hutchinson, Brian. "Restored 'Theatre of Risks,'" *The Financial Post*, 20 March 1993, S5.

Knowles, Richard Paul. "Replaying History: Canadian Historiography and Metadrama," *Dalhousie Review*, 67:2/3 (1987).

Pollock, Sharon. *Fair Liberty's Call.* unpublished MS.

Pollock, Sharon. *The Komagata Maru Incident.* Toronto: Playwright's Co-op, 1978.

Pollock, Sharon. *Walsh.* Vancouver: Talonbooks, 1973.

Rudakoff, Judith and Rita Much. *Fair Play: 12 Women Speak.* Toronto: Simon and Pierre, 1990.

Wallace, Robert and Cynthia Zimmerman, *The Work: Conversations with English-Canadian Playwrights.* Toronto: Coach House, 1982.

Broken Toys

The Destruction of the National Hero in the Early History Plays of Sharon Pollock

Heidi J. Holder

In the burst of theatrical activity in the Canada of the 1970s, one finds a notably high number of historical dramas. The focus on history is not altogether surprising; much of the innovative theatrical work during this period was self-consciously "Canadian," preoccupied with issues of identity and nationalism. This increase in play production formed part of a general increase in activity – supported and prodded on by the government – in the domestic cultural arena; numerous theatre companies, theatre festivals, journals, and publishing houses appeared on the scene, devoted to the examination and delineation of a domestic – as opposed to a colonial or American – identity and mentality. Theatre critic Don Rubin, recalling his work as a drama critic in the early 1970s, notes that "in Canada 'alternate theatre' came simply to be associated with the production of work . . . by *Canadian* authors. And *Canadian* was the key" (16). Rubin finds in many of the history plays of the time "a sense of national dignity and national celebration" (21). The sense of Canadian theatre as a "novelty" or wonder has since subsided, but the plays of this period offer a useful case study of the intersection of theatrical technique and cultural politics; in particular, the plays of Sharon Pollock reveal the peculiar nature of the "national celebration" to be found on the Canadian stage in the 1970s. In *Walsh* (Theatre Calgary 1973) and *The Komagata Maru Incident* (Vancouver Playhouse 1976) Pollock stages the collapse of two "national heroes," in plays dealing respectively with the Sioux crisis of the 1870s and ethnic hostilities in 1914 Vancouver.

In the decade following the celebration of the centennial of Confederation in 1967, the Canadian theatregoer would see an astonishing array of specifically Canadian historical subjects represented by playwrights and companies: Théâtre Passe Muraille's *The Doukhobors* (1971) and *Them Donnellys* (1973); Carol Bolt's *Buffalo Jump* (Théâtre Passe Muraille 1972); James Reaney's *Donnelly* trilogy at the Tarragon Theatre – *Sticks and Stones* (1973), *The St. Nicholas Hotel* (1974), and *Handcuffs* (1975); James W. Nichol's *Sainte-Marie Among the Hurons* (Theatre London 1974); Rick Salutin's collaboration with Theatre Passe Muraille on *1837: The Farmer's Revolt* (1974) and his own "hockey night" version of the history of French- and Anglo-Canadian conflict in *Les Canadiens* (1977); Herschel Hardin's *The Great Wave of Civilization* (Festival Lennoxville 1976), and John Gray and Eric Peterson's *Billy Bishop goes to War* (1978). It is curious to note that the subject matter chosen by playwrights and collaborative companies was not necessarily flattering to a Canadian audience. In the above list (which records only part of the dramatic output of the time), an audience might see the following images from their past: the intolerance faced by immigrant groups; the suffering brought by European immigrants to such native peoples as the Huron and the Blackfeet; a notorious mass murder inspired by religious and ethnic conflict; the suppression of popular rebellions fomented by victims of economic injustices; and the disillusionment of a national war hero. Salutin's *Les Canadiens*, ending as it does with the victory of the Parti Québécois in 1976, is arguably the most "upbeat" of the plays, although it too is firmly focused on notions and images of defeat and cultural conflict.

Given this preoccupation with the darker aspects of history, Pollock's plays do not appear unusual in their choice of unpleasant or difficult subject matter. Margaret Atwood, in her early but still useful *Survival: A Thematic Guide to Canadian Literature* (1972), offers a witty, half-serious overview of the importance of failure and defeat in Canadian culture: "Canadians," she notes, "show a marked preference for the negative" (35). The taste for defeat and disaster certainly seems in evidence in the theatre of the 1970s. But one must ask what the audience experiences and takes away from such performances. And the answer to that question, I think, varies widely. In both *Walsh* and *The Komagata Maru Incident* playwright Sharon Pollock sets her sights on representative male figures from Canadian history: James A. Walsh, the superintendent of the N.W.M.P., a Canadian Institution of heroic repute; and Inspector William Hopkinson, an official in the Immigration Department, an institution that played (and plays) a crucial role in defining the national character. In *Walsh* the focus is on the title character's role in the return of Sitting Bull and the Sioux to the United States in the 1870s. In *The Komagata Maru Incident* Inspector William Hopkinson works feverishly but ambivalently to keep a boatload of Sikhs (who in fact have the right of entry into Canada) from disembarking in Vancouver in 1914 (the operation was successful, and only 20 of the 376 passengers were allowed to enter the country).

Pollock's choice of historical subjects reveals both a broad historical perspective and a narrow, rather perverse dramatic method: a complicated historical background is often forsaken for a highly focused and subjective analysis of one individual. A more common approach in the history plays of the 1970s was to rely on an ensemble (especially in the collectively-created pieces), eschewing a sharp focus on one character. A picture of a group – ethnic, racial, religious – emerges; but in Pollock's plays we see an individual in conflict not only with a group of "outsiders," but also with the group of which, ostensibly, he is a part. Pollock's choice of method here is neither careless nor accidental, and merits closer analysis.

The historical subjects of both *Walsh* and *The Komagata Maru Incident* are immensely complicated, involving diverse interests that are local, national, and international. In the case of *Walsh*, the hegira of Sitting Bull and the Sioux in Canada following the Battle of Little Big Horn provoked a five-year battle of wills among the Canadian, U.S., and British governments, the leaders of the Sioux and other native nations, and the military authorities in the west of Canada and the United States. Coming soon after the Confederation, the "problem" of the non-Canadian Sioux can be seen as a test of the authority of the Dominion government. Cynthia Zimmerman comments on the "Canadian" nature of the problematic relationship between Walsh and the Sioux, noting that "Walsh's experience of being used by his superiors, his final recognition that he, like the Sioux, is only a pawn in a much bigger game that has little to do with justice, seems quintessentially colonial" (68). Similarly complex, the "problem" of the Komagata Maru involved the Canadian, U.S., British, and Indian governments, a politically divided Sikh community, and a Japanese-owned ship.

Both cases also involved outsiders claiming status as insiders. When the Sioux arrived in Canada they asserted their right to the protection of the Crown since they had fought on the British side in the War of 1812; they also reminded the Canadians that their government had given refuge to the Santee Sioux following the Minnesota war in the 1860s (Manzione 44, Turner 52). In Pollock's *Walsh* this claim is made by the chief Gall immediately upon the introduction of Walsh to the Sioux:

> My grandfather was a soldier for the grandfather of Queen Victoria. At that time your people told him that the Sioux nation belonged to that grandfather of the Queen. My people fought against the Longknives for your people then. We were told that you would always look after your red children. Now the Longknives have stolen our land. We have no place to go. We come home to you asking for that protection you promised (40).

The stage direction indicates that "Walsh is not actually prepared for this specific argument for Canada's obligation to the Sioux." The Sikhs aboard the Komagata Maru insisted upon their rights as British subjects to travel anywhere within the empire. The leader of the expedition, Gurdit Singh, had this to say to the Vancouver press when the ship arrived in harbour:

> We are British citizens and we insist that we have a right to visit any part of the Empire . . . We are determined to make this a test case and if we are refused entrance into your country, the matter will not end here." (Johnston 37-8)

Further complicating matters, some of the men on board were veterans of the Indian army, and had therefore served the Crown.

A further similarity between the two historical events lies in the nature of the "outsiders'" defeat. In both cases Canada eventually rid itself of the unwanted immigrants by tedious legalistic and/or diplomatic maneuvering and deprivation of supplies. The Sioux and the Sikhs both stubbornly endured appalling living conditions rather than return to homelands where they were unwelcome and threatened with incarceration or death. In both cases, in fact, they received exactly the reception they feared: the turned-back passengers of the Komagata Maru, some of them members of the revolutionary Ghadr [mutiny] Party, rioted at Budge Budge, where twelve of them were killed; Sitting Bull and those who surrendered with him, promised a place at the Standing Rock Agency (in North Dakota), were removed from there to Fort Buford, where they were interned as prisoners of war for nearly two years (Turner 250-51). The defeats inflicted on the Sioux and the Sikhs were not, despite the self-congratulatory rhetoric of much of the contemporary press, especially glorious. In short, both plays are about successes of the young Dominion government, successes which time has diminished and redefined. These dramas of resistance and expulsion have as their subjects historical events that could, in the earlier melodramatic style of the late nineteenth and early twentieth centuries, have been treated as part of an heroic national mythology. In the 1970s, when the terms of public debate over racial and ethnic issues had been considerably altered, these subjects were obvious candidates for revision.

Given the complexity of this material, Pollock's handling of it is surprising. In both cases she limits the setting.

Despite the wide range of potential players and settings, she maintains a fairly consistent unity of place, even at the cost of inaccuracy. *Walsh* is set at and around Fort Walsh, in the Cypress Hills of the Northwest Territories. The exception here is the Prologue, set in the Yukon in 1890, which is discussed below. A sharply divergent treatment of the same subject is found in Ken Mitchell's *The Medicine Line* (winner of the Drama for Saskatchewan Heritage competition, 1974), in which the scene ranges from Fort Walsh to Ottawa and Queen Victoria's reception room in London. So determined is Pollock to restrict the setting that she even shows Walsh receiving the news of Sitting Bull's violent death while still in command of Fort Walsh, when in fact he was in Winnipeg running a coal business when he read a newspaper account of the killing (Turner 260-63).

The setting of *The Komagata Maru Incident* is somewhat more ambiguous, but still quite limited. Much of the play takes place in a brothel, where Inspector Hopkinson lives with his prostitute-lover Evy; other characters seen here are Sophie, another prostitute, and Georg, a German national. The relationships among these characters are tense and occasionally hostile. Around the brothel setting is an "arc or runway" where Hopkinson plays his scenes with another character, T.S. The latter is a sort of Master of Ceremonies who also plays the part of Hopkinson's generic "superior"; in fact, he stands in for such historical figures as Vancouver immigration agent Malcolm R. J. Reid, Conservative Member of Parliament. H.H. Stevens, and B.C. Premier Sir Richard McBride. The passengers are represented by a Sikh woman, a widow, on a level above and behind the main area; she is behind a cage-like frame and speaks intermittently to a child whom we do not see.

By using T.S. to represent a kind of generic officialdom, Pollock avoids any precise characterization or recreation. He is a floating, menacing, even ahistorical voice of authority. Other "voices" are left out altogether. J. Edward Bird, the indefatigable lawyer for the passengers, is not so much as mentioned; the Sikh community in Vancouver, highly active on both sides of the crisis, is not embodied on the stage; and the passengers themselves are represented by one figure who is flatly unhistorical, since the only two women on the Komagata Maru were travelling with their husbands. The most notable omission from among the passengers is the charismatic revolutionary Gurdit Singh, who organized the voyage but is not so much as mentioned by name in the play. The brothel and its inhabitants are fictitious. One could easily imagine more clearly "documentary" approaches to this subject. One reviewer, in fact, suggested that "rightfully, the play should have concentrated on [the] conspiracy between immigration department officials and the police" (Freeman).

Pollock's highly idiosyncratic use of the material in these two plays indicates that her interest lies not *primarily* in the conflict among different nations, factions, or ethnic groups. Her focus is on the men in the middle, the administrators or investigators, who function in the area between the power of governments and the resistance of the unwanted, would-be immigrants. Both of these characters were in their time considered heroic figures. As Jamie Portman noted in his review of *Walsh* at Theatre Calgary, "All of us learned of this event at school" (cited in Conolly 136). Walsh's reputation (he was a more flamboyant figure in contemporary accounts than in Pollock's play) rested on the notion that he could "control" Sitting Bull and the Sioux. In a famous but apocryphal incident of this period, Walsh knocked down Sitting Bull during an argument over food supplies, and booted him out the door of his office. Similarly, Hopkinson was considered by many white Canadians to be a hero and martyr, a man with "special knowledge" of the Sikhs and their ways.

In Pollock's plays the central male figures fail to grow into heroes, instead gradually losing their sense of identity. Although *Walsh* chronicles the suffering and fate of Sitting Bull, the Hunkpapa Sioux, and the Nez Perce, this is *not* what we see. Pollock instead places before us the destruction of Walsh as a man and administrator. The focus shifts from the obvious victim – the Native Americans – to the local representative of the government, forced to implement policies he opposes. The dramatist wants us to recognize that Walsh and most of his men are not villains; this point and Pollock's technique are clear in the Nez Perce scene, when, instead of actually seeing the few members of the tribe who made it across the border, we seen the reactions of the Canadians:

> Walsh looks at Sitting Bull and then off at the sound of people approaching. The light begins to flicker as if people were passing in front of it, Walsh turns slowly looking outside the light. There is a muffled sound of people moaning. A blue light picks out Clarence [the young recruit] as he makes his way towards Walsh (57).

Clarence, the character whose attitude towards the Sioux undergoes the greatest transformation, wants to give his coat to freezing children, and asks, "will the government mind about the coat?" The gesture is clearly a useless one at this point. Walsh had previously asked Sitting Bull to deny help to the Nez Perce, who wanted the Sioux to help them fight their way to Canada; in turn, Walsh will be told by the government in Ottawa to deny aid to the Sioux (they are denied provisions by the Canadian government) in order to force them back into the U.S. What we see is an endless series of betrayals, to no clear purpose. The only people we see are, to a greater or lesser extent, losers.

Again, the issue of perspective arises. Pollock is not simply concerned with Canada's treatment of Indians, but with Canada's standing as a nation. National identity was a common topic of interest in the 1970s, for playwrights, critics, and audiences. The theatrical response to an historical subject often included commentary on its relevance to the present political and cultural situation. Rick Salutin recalls that in the development of *1837* the actors drew upon their own resentments "against British imperialism in the contemporary theatre" (Bessai, *Playwrights* 37-38); Diane Bessai suggests that *The Doukhobours*, with its focus on resistance to assimilation, played on anti-authoritarian feeling in the wake of the Quebec crisis (*Playwrights* 51); and W.H. New has said, of the plays of the 1970s, that

> such works do not interest themselves in what historians have received as 'fact' so much as they seek to reinterpret or reclaim the past from one particular interpretation of it, with an eye on some present tension (252-53).

New may be overstating the playwrights' lack of interest in facts, but he is surely on target in his assertion that their goal is often to reinterpret the "successes" or "failures" of the past.

The disgrace in *Walsh* is not simply in what one does, but in what one is bullied into doing. Sitting Bull turns his back on the Nez Perce, Walsh and the N.W.M.P. turn their backs on the Sioux, the government in Ottawa turns its back on Walsh. The international maneuvering during the Sioux's residence in Canada, caused in large part by the conflicting interests of a U.S. government that both desired revenge on the Sioux and rejected responsibility for them, made Walsh's knowledge and expertise irrelevant. This situation is clear in an exchange between Walsh and his supervisor:

> WALSH. What about my recommendations concerning the Indians?
> MACLEOD. What about them?
> WALSH. The Sioux have as much legal right to a reservation here, as the Santee Sioux had in Manitoba.
> MACLEOD. The Santee Sioux did not kill Custer.
> WALSH. They killed over six hundred white settlers in Minnesota who were not engaged in an act of war against them. Why are my recommendations not acted upon?
> MACLEOD. Out here you don't see the whole picture. There are other considerations (84-5).

According to Pollock's interpretation, in Walsh Canada has not created a hero so much as destroyed one. As Herbert Whittaker noted in his review of the 1974 production at Third Stage in Stratford, the play "is an account of international relationships transcending human ones." The failure to incorporate the Sioux into Canada results in the disintegration of its representative figure.

Walsh's frustrations finally reduce him to a brute when he knocks down, kicks, and humiliates Sitting Bull. Pollock makes much of this apocryphal episode. Although it takes place late in the play, we actually *see* it earlier, replayed with different figures. In the dreamlike Prologue, Walsh is the drunken, broken Commissioner of the Yukon. When asked by a prospector (the same actor plays Sitting Bull) for some money for Joie the newspaper boy (the same actor plays Bull's son Crowfoot), Walsh shouts repeatedly, "I can give you nothing" – his words to Sitting Bull before their altercation. When Walsh knocks down the prospector, the voice of Clarence the recruit screams from offstage, "Nooooooooo!" (13) – just as he will when Walsh knocks down Bull later in the play (101).

The audience watching the prologue cannot understand the significance of this scene until very late in the play. The ultimate effect is of a character trapped in a nightmare of helpless repetition. The Prologue was, in fact, added only when Pollock revised the play for production at Stratford in 1974, and Herbert Whittaker, reviewing the revised version, accurately observes its intended effect:

> we worry that the drama of Walsh will not get started, only to discover it already has, and that we are now becoming aware of the dreadful inevitability of it. We are offered no false hope, only solemn steps toward a kind of doom.

The original version of the play had, instead of the Prologue, speeches from contemporary sources read aloud before each of the twelve scenes. Pollock's decision to delete the speeches and add the Prologue shifts the emphasis to one defining action, a moment that traps Walsh and makes manifest the hidden brutality of the Canadian government's policies toward the Sioux.

Pollock's choices here tell us something about her view of the relationship between fact and fiction in historical drama. Pollock has selected, as a critical moment for Walsh and the play, an event that is patently "mythic" in quality and dubious in authenticity. If in this play she has, as Zimmerman, suggests, "targeted our myth of the glorious mounties" (67), she has also attempted to convey truth through a rather teasing use of the possibly-untrue, of mythic roles and types. Likewise in *The Komagata Maru Incident* Pollock again chooses to focus on a historically questionable "fact" – in this case, that Inspector William Hopkinson was part Indian. Hugh Johnston offers a useful analysis of Hopkinson's odd "position": an Inspector with the Calcutta Metropolitan Police, Hopkinson was on leave but working as a spy in the United States and Canada for the Indian government, and given a position in the Canadian Immigration Branch (7-8, 10-11). Johnston also addresses, in a footnote, the rumour that Hopkinson's mother was Indian (142-3). Pollock has latched onto this rumour and made it the central motivating force for Hopkinson. As with Walsh, by expelling a group labelled "the enemy," Hopkinson engages in a doomed effort to maintain a sense of identity, to deny his own connection and identification with a despised group.

While being harassed by T.S., who demands new ideas for getting rid of the ship's passengers, Hopkinson feels compelled to describe to his mistress Evy his first meeting with Mewa Singh, the man who will later assassinate him. Mewa Singh was imprisoned for gun-running and Hopkinson was trying to recruit him as an informant. Something in Mewa Singh's look, he said, had reminded him of a time when he was a child in India, standing in a desolate bazaar the day after a massacre:

> I saw a figure approaching from one of the streets. Some native person. He stopped in the shadow of the

huts... he extended his arms t'wards me ... and I ... turned around... and ran home (20).

Later, when Evy taunts Hopkinson about his origins – "funny thing, your background," says Evy (32) – we learn of the possibility that he is part Indian. "Billy's mother's Brown!" she chants, until Hopkinson slaps her. The earlier childhood reminiscence takes on a difference interpretation; it represents not so much the fear or shame of an English child, as the rejection by an Anglo-Indian child of his mother's kind.

Late in the play Hopkinson, discussing the coming war with a German national eager to turn spy, denies that he is in any way like the German:

> In this stinking world there's two kinds, there's the ruler and the ruled – when I see the likes of you, I know where I stand! (he begins to weaken) Some people talk, and some people listen, but by God, I act, and if ... it weren't for people like me ... people like you would be down in the slime ... I have my ... I have my ... (43-44).

As with Walsh, Hopkinson ultimately cannot articulate a philosophy that gives any real meaning to his actions.

Both Walsh and Hopkinson find themselves dehumanized, reduced to mechanical men helplessly reenacting the past. When Walsh has returned to the Fort after being summoned east, Sitting Bull has already returned to the U.S. and Walsh is now taking up his role and "playing Indian" for easterners celebrating the opening of a new stretch of railroad (See Nunn, "Sharon Pollock's Plays," 74). A subordinate brings in a "large board, on it a map with toy soldiers, a train engine, tree." What at first sounds like plans for authentic military action is revealed, as Walsh continues, to be an entertaining "stunt":

> WALSH. Right! I will ride out of the woods. my men behind me, and all of us in full dress – tell the men to practice war whoops. I want good full-blooded Indian yells, you hear?
> McCUTCHEON. Aye Sir.
> WALSH. So out we come – yelling bloody murder – I'll swing aboard the train and ride it into Calgary. Well, what do you think? Is that a stirring sight or not?
> McCUTCHEON. Very stirring, sir.
> WALSH. When you open a railroad, you do it in style, I say! Bloody train will be full of easterners and we'll scare the pants off every one of them. I want a good show (114).

Shortly after this exchange, Walsh receives the news of Sitting Bull's death. Ironically, his fate here seems similar to that of the Sioux chief, who was also reduced to playing in sham "reenactments" in Buffalo Bill's Wild West Show. Walsh is trapped between the identities of ruler and ruled. His identification with Bull is balanced by his adoption of the brutal manner of the government, and he is compelled to relive that role, haunted by his humiliation of the chief.

Walsh's confusion as to his role or identity is apparent in a number of scenes: when General MacLeod tells him "you play chess – sometimes a pawn is sacrificed on one side of the board to gain an advantage on the other," Walsh responds with disbelief, "I am a pawn?" (85). MacLeod assures him that he was referring to Sitting Bull, but Walsh's confusion on this point is telling. Later in this confrontation Walsh asks MacLeod, "What do you think happens when I take off this tunic?": "Do you think McCutcheon hangs me from some god damn wooden peg with my strings dangling? . . . Do you think I'm a puppet? Manipulate me and anything is possible" (86). The "costume" of the NWMP is used to good effect in a number of scenes (Salter 16). In the encounter with the Nez Perce survivors, Walsh removes his tunic so that it might be given to a freezing woman; when she turns out to be dead, Clarence hands it back to him, and he lets it drop to the ground. Louis, a Métis scout, tells him that "you can't just throw it away, sir. Dat's too easy" (58). In the play's final scene, when Walsh has heard of the death of Sitting Bull, he removes the tunic and lays it across the desk. The business with the tunic, the puppet imagery, Walsh's confusion of himself with Sitting Bull, and the plans for the "wild Indians" show all contribute to a sense of Walsh as a figure lacking – or resisting – an identity. In a sad irony, Walsh has become a puppet for the government.

Hopkinson also feels compelled to take up the "role" of his victims: Evy notes that he "gets himself all dolled up, goes to the temple in disguise" (32) – something Hopkinson was in fact alleged to have done as a spy. The emphasis on role-playing is intensified in this play by the presence of T.S., whose identity in fact shifts constantly. The emcee makes the play's travesty of heroism clear, as he addresses his underlings in the Immigration Office:

> *(Howls on his haunches, boy scout position, two fingers of each hand at temples.)* Akela says, "Be prepared." *(Howls.)* Akela says, "Do your duty for God and the King, and Obey the Law of the Pack." *(Howls, then stops abruptly and rises.)* Akela says, "I have three merits badges for the boy who comes up with a first-rate reason to board the Komagata Maru!" (26)

One "role" for Hopkinson to play, apparently, was boy scout.

The play also makes significant use of the "toy" or "puppet" image. As the moment of his death approaches, Hopkinson will compare himself to a toy, a mechanical man:

> I leave the house early. I walk to the court house . . . It's Fall . . . I feel like a toy man walking through a toy town. Everything's working. My arms and my legs move so well together there is . . . a mechanical precision to everything . . . I notice the houses seem neater than usual, a certain precision . . . at the same time, it's slower, things are slower, but very precise . . . toy mountains frame my toy town (46).

At the courthouse, while waiting to testify on behalf of his informant Bela Singh (who had opened fire at radical Sikhs in a gurdwara, killing two and wounding ten), Hopkinson sees Mewa Singh, who is about to assassinate him: "When I see him, I feel myself bursting. My toy town is destroyed in an instant" (47). In Pollock's play Hopkinson actually embraces his assassin, reversing the lifelong rejection of his Indian identity. Caught between his identification with "the ruler and the ruled," Hopkinson dies a most ironic death.

Other aspects of Pollock's dramatic technique contribute to the sense of identity under stress. In both plays Pollock indicates that there are to be no blackouts; one scene should blend into the next. Even the Prologue of *Walsh* should move directly into the first act of the play, the result being a more fluid sense of time and a lack of pause or relief between scenes. Pollock has complained that directors often ignore these instructions with regard to *Walsh*, tending to "stage it as an historical pageant"

(Wallace and Zimmerman 116). Attempting to avoid such problems with *The Komagata Maru Incident*, she used a "circus" apparatus, with T.S. presiding; "the characters," she instructs, "never leave the stage" (production note in text). Robert Nunn has examined Pollock's use of "montage," "the juxtaposition of scenes in different styles," without breaks or blackouts. He suggests that this technique is partly due to the need to "get certain things into the play" ("Sharon Pollock's Plays" 75), but the effect can also be one of unstoppable action, of action that shifts quickly in tone or meaning, of action that traps the central figure. The manipulation of the sense of time in the plays suggests the mental stress suffered by Walsh and Hopkinson; the structure often seems determined by their fears and anxieties. This is particularly true in *Walsh*, where the entire play proper can be seen as an extended flashback in the older Walsh's mind.

In her later historical dramas, Pollock would continue to employ self-consciously "theatrical" devices; she would also maintain her focus on the symbolic or mythic individual. Interestingly, her choice of central characters shifts to murderers even as the importance of gender increases in her plays. In *Blood Relations* (Theatre 3, Edmonton 1980), her retelling of the Lizzie Borden story, Lizzie responds to a request for the "truth" by staging her own story: she plays director and her actress-companion plays "Lizzie." The fascination with the connection between the mode and the material – between the "theatrical" and the "true" – remains central. When Lizzie's sister asks if she committed the crimes (and it is clear in this version that she did), Lizzie responds by using theatrical imagery to shift responsibility:

> Did you ever stop to think that if I did, then you were guilty too? . . . Did you ever stop and think that I was like a puppet, your puppet. My hand your hand, yes, your hand working my mouth, me saying all the things you felt like saying, me doing all the things you felt like doing (70).

In *Saucy Jack* (Garry Theatre, Calgary 1993), Pollock's Jack-the-Ripper play, the shading between the roles of victim and "director" are even more slippery. An actress has been hired by J. K. Stephen ("Jem"), an apparently unbalanced friend and tutor of Prince Albert Victor (known as "Eddy"); she is to help him reenact the deaths of the Ripper's victims for the Prince and another "guest," Montague Druitt. The actress, Kate, seems to be a prop in a dangerous game of guilt and potential blackmail among the men, but she is ultimately able to walk away alive – which cannot be said of all the male characters. Pollock's take on the Ripper mystery uses several of the traditional suspects: Druitt, Prince Eddy, and Stephen.

In both of these history/crime dramas, the playwright shows even more strongly than in the historical dramas of the 1970s her penchant for manipulating tales, speculation, and myth; both *Blood Relations* and *Saucy Jack* toy with our simultaneous desire for knowledge and love of fictionalizing and myth-making. It is not by accident that she chose, as historical subjects of feminist revisionism, two of the most lurid and bedeviling mysteries in Victorian crime. Pollock sees in the difficult distinction between fact and fiction an opportunity to present an audience not only with facts (and the problem of identifying them), but also with the significance and costs of our own desire to create meaning out of them, to find a coherent story or message in the fragments of history. Pollock pushes the audience to consider the *sources* of facts, which are all too often the mythologizing authorities, embodied in *The Komagata Maru Incident*, for instance, by the character T.S.

Richard Paul Knowles, commenting on *Blood Relations*, observes that "for Pollock the 'facts' . . . are less important than the imaginative truth, the past that we must allow ourselves to imagine and therefore to bring into being as part of our present" (240). It is in her fascination with the process of history-making that Pollock challenges her audience. Although her history plays of the 1970s were part of a larger trend in which the theatre was used to examine significant incidents and problems in Canadian history, Pollock's work was arguably less pleasant for the audience than most. Knowles has argued that in the productions of Pollock, Salutin, and Reaney we can see an emphasis on the "role of the audience in the 'realization' of the past" (237); his analysis here is based on the use of metatheatric devices. In Pollock's plays these devices do not serve so much to join the audience with the actors and playwright in a recreation of "their" history, as to put them in an uncomfortable "dual" role as audience. The determined, sometimes desperate theatricalizing of events and personalities in *Walsh* and *The Komagata Maru Incident* is closely tied to the disintegration of the main characters, their reduction to toy figures. Their role-playing both facilitates and represents their destruction; moreover, such role-playing implies an audience, and, since the sources of real power are usually offstage in Pollock's plays, the audience bears much of the burden.

The idea of an audience, of spectators, assumes a rather sinister quality in Pollock's work. We may not wish to be identified with the concept of audience put forth *within* the plays, but that role is foisted on us nonetheless.

Robert Nunn has suggested that the character T.S. in *The Komagata Maru Incident* places us in the uncomfortable position of being addressed as part of the white population of 1914 Vancouver:

> as audience we are alienated from an automatic acceptance of the predominance of "the White Race" . . . the play forces us to either criticize or justify the state of affairs: we cannot take it for granted ("Performing Fact" 56).

If such history plays encourage, in Knowles's words, an "active and on-going engagement with the imagination and the will," we are also forced to see the dangers inherent in the on-going, communal creation of history: the imagination can create destructive myths (as in T.S.'s tale-spinning and Walsh's play-acting) just as easily as constructive ones.

This heightened sense of the possibilities – often dangerous, sometimes liberating – of adopting a "role" would remain central to Pollock's dramatic technique. Both *Blood Relations* and *Saucy Jack* would make use of characters who were, in fact, actresses. In these plays, "acting" is a way to reveal or avoid the truth. This theatrical sensibility would remain when Pollock returned to Canadian historical themes in 1993 with *Fair Liberty's Call* (Stratford Festival). Here Pollock revisits another cherished Canadian myth, that of the welcoming of the loyalists who fled the United States after the Revolution and settled in New Brunswick. The play, set after the war's end, is overwhelmingly concerned with the burden of the past – all of the characters are fixated on past betrayals and sufferings. The events unfold during a gathering of veterans of "Tarleton's Loyalist Legion"; the characters attempt to celebrate the past, but the past itself keeps intruding, as a visitor (loyalist? rebel?) shows up seeking vengeance for a massacre. Outrages committed by both loyalists and rebels – massacres at Cherry Valley, Waxhaws, Cowpens – continue to bear effects.

The "celebration" that is the framing event of the play constantly threatens to fall to pieces under the weight of factionalism, guilt, and disappointed hopes. It also provides another of Pollock's self-consciously metatheatrical devices, as characters set the stage and put on costumes for the event:

> Major Williams, George, and Daniel begin to drag out the totems, souvenirs, and trophies of war from tru[n]ks, boxes, and containers. They will decorate both the space and themselves as they prepare for the Remembrance Ritual (36-37).

The pattern adopted in the play is one of ordered celebration of the past interrupted by unresolved conflicts and injustices of the past. The presence of "Eddie" intensifies the theatricality of the piece: this character, a veteran of Tarleton's Legion, is really a female, "Emily," who adopted her brother's "role" as loyalist soldier after he committed suicide. This most recent of Pollock's history plays shows her continued reliance on metatheatric technique, and on characters' apparently inevitable reiteration of lines and actions. As Nothof notes

> cycles of bloody reprisals run through the play: everything goes round and round. The boots of a dead rebel are taken by a loyalist soldier, and in turn taken by another rebel (482).

This later work, however, shows a shift in emphasis away from a single representative and *historical* character. The intense scrutiny of a well-known national figure is a tactic limited to the early historical dramas. Pollock herself has commented usefully on the structure of her plays:

> I think I write the same play over and over again. It is a play about an individual who is directed to or compelled to follow a course of action of which he or she begins to examine the morality. Circumstances force a decision, usually the authority (family, society, government) is removed emotionally or geographically from the protagonist, and it usually doesn't end very well (Much 210).

This fascination with individual decisions, as it appears in *Walsh* and *The Komagata Maru Incident* is striking in the context of much of the historical drama of the 1970s, which tended to examine the collision of "groups" rather than the actions of individuals. Pollock's choice of focus could be judged "old-fashioned," one more in line with traditional history plays. The traditional, received and accepted versions of things are exactly what attract the playwright, and she has a surprising way of using them. She shows their making, their enduring power, and our own complicity in their creation and vitality.

Pollock's history plays of the 1970s are traditional history plays inverted: rather than depicting heroic lives they detail the failure of the "heroic." In analyzing Pollock's domestic plays, Bessai has asserted that "the recurring pattern in the plays . . . is of individual struggle against a social or political order of which the character is a part" ("Women Dramatists" 106). The same could be said of the earlier history plays, in which the crucial conflict is an internal one. Both of Pollock's "heroes" of the 1970s are mechanical men, in that they helplessly follow the policies of their governments; but they are, instead of national heroes, simply self-destruct mechanisms. This emphasis on the would-be "heroic" figure is, arguably, a useful approach to injustices of the past. The audience with knowledge of the history of the Sioux or the passengers on the Komagata Maru will fully expect that those people will be the losers; Sitting Bull will die and the Sikhs will be sent back to India. Part of the burden of the genre of the history play is that audiences often know the stories. Pollock plays with audience expectations, mixing a great deal of information with a perverse fictionalizing of her central character; she thus directs the audience's attention to another set of "losers" entirely.

Bessai has commented on the "documentary element" present in much of the Canadian drama of the 1970s, suggesting that it represents an attempt to "develop dramatic forms appropriate to the many hitherto neglected areas of this country's subject matter" ("Canadian Docu-Drama" 7). By combining documentary elements with a marked fictionalizing of her central characters – a fictionalizing more in keeping with "old-fashioned" dramas than with the "new" docu-drama of the 1970s – Pollock's work is designed to draw our attention to the connections between fact and myth in Canada's past. Salter has suggested, not quite with admiration, that *The Komagata Maru Incident* has "all the trappings of a history play" (xvi), and his observation says much about the discomfiting presence of traditional elements in Pollock's plays. They are inevitably intended to draw attention to themselves, to their own importance in the creation of an historical mythology that Pollock simultaneously exploits and undermines; the playwright points up both the strong attraction and the inevitable danger inherent in the storytelling that creates a version of history, and she does so at a time when the construction of a Canadian identity and history was very much in vogue.

In Pollock's reading, Walsh and Hopkinson are undone rather than exalted by their own myths. They are "despairing individuals" (Wallace and Zimmerman 121), and are also "Canadian" in a way the Sioux and the Sikhs were not permitted to be.

Notes

1   The passenger roster of the Komagata Maru listed 376 passengers: 24 Muslims, 12 Hindus, and 340 Sikhs. Most of the passengers came from villages on the Panjab plain.

2   For a useful discussion of Pollock's critique of the idea of "borders," see Nothof.

3   For analysis of this lengthy diplomatic crisis and the resulting return of the Sioux to the United States, see Joyner, Manzione and Turner.

4   The handling of the Komagata Maru's passengers and the national and international effects of their expulsion have received considerable attention from historians. Hugh Johnston's definitive *The Voyage of the "Komagata Maru"* remains the best source; also noteworthy are Ted Ferguson's *A White Man's Country*, and *Beyond the Komagata Maru: Race Relations Today* (proceedings of a 1989 conference organized by the Progressive Indo-Canadian Community Services Society, Surrey, B.C.). For the perspective of Indian historians on the event, see Lal, and Vidyarthi.

5   Johnston explains the forced disembarkation at Budge Budge thus: "The state of war, unemployment in Calcutta, and the suspected *Ghadr* connection with the ship were all the excuse that the Indian authorities needed to use the new Ingress to India Ordinance against the passengers of the Komagata Maru. In consultation with the government of the Panjab and the Government of India, the local government of Bengal decided to take the passengers off at Budge Budge, before they reached Calcutta, and to transport most of them by train at government expense to their homes in the Panjab, arresting and detaining any who appeared to be agitators. A party of Panjab police were sent to Calcutta to be on hand when the ship arrived" (96).

6   It is unclear whether this "fight" actually occurred, but it has become an enduring part of the myths surrounding Walsh and Sitting Bull. In his account of this incident, Turner attributes the whole thing to exhaustion on Walsh's part and desperation on Sitting Bull's (201-02). Manzione, however, notes the lack of reliable sources for this story. That the event remains a popular piece of the mythology surrounding the NWMP is evident in history texts and children's literature (see, for example, Leeder 48-9).

7   Hopkinson remains a hero in some quarters, in particular among those opposed to Asian immigrants. For a useful example see Jarvis. Jarvis's text was published by the Citizens for Foreign Aid Reform, a British Columbia-based pro-Apartheid and anti-immigrant group; Jarvis himself is a founding member of the William Hopkinson Society.

8   This interpretation of Hopkinson's parentage still holds credence. Nothof, for instance, accepts it as fact (480).

WORKS CITED

Atwood, Margaret. *Survival: A Thematic Guide to Canadian Literature.* Toronto: Anansi, 1972.

Bessai, Diane. "Canadian Docu-drama." *Canadian Theatre Review* 16 (Fall 1977): 7-10.

—. *Playwrights of Collective Creation. The Canadian Dramatist* 2. Toronto: Simon & Pierre 1992.

—. "Women Dramatists: Sharon Pollock and Judith Thompson." *Post Colonial English Drama.* Ed. Bruce King. New York: St. Martin's, 1992. 97-117.

Beyond the Komagata Maru: Race Relations Today. Surrey, B.C.: Progressive Indo-Canadian Community Services Society, 1990.

Conolly, L. W., ed.. *Canadian Drama and the Critics.* Vancouver: Talonbooks, 1987.

Ferguson, Ted. *A White Man's Country: An Exercise in Canadian Prejudice.* Toronto: Doubleday, 1975.

Freeman, Brian. "In Review: *The Komagata Maru Incident.*" *Scene Changes* 5:9 (December 1977): 20-21.

Jarvis, Robert. *The "Komagata Maru" Incident: A Canadian Immigration Battle Revisited.* Toronto: Citizens for Foreign Aid Reform, 1992. C-FAR Canadian Issues Series 32.

Johnston, Hugh J.M. *The Voyage of the Komagata Maru: The Sikh Challenge to Canada's Colour Bar*. Delhi: Oxford UP, 1979.

Joyner, Christopher C. "The Hegira of Sitting Bull to Canada: Diplomatic Realpolitik, 1876-1881." *Journal of the West* 13 (April 1974): 6-18.

Knowles, Richard Paul. "Replaying History: Canadian Historiographic Metadrama." *Dalhousie Review* 67 (Summer/Fall 1987): 228-43.

Lal, Bru V. "Political Movement in the Early East Indian Community in Canada." *Journal of Indian History* 58:1-3 (1980): 193-220.

Leeder, Terry. *White Forehead of the Cypress Hills*. Toronto: Dundurn, 1979.

Manzione, Joseph. *"I am Looking to the North for My Life": Sitting Bull, 1876-1881*. Salt Lake City: U of Utah P, 1991.

Much, Rita. "Sharon Pollock Interview." *Fair Play: 12 Women Speak. Conversations with Canadian Playwrights*. Eds. Judith Rudakoff and Rita Much. Toronto: Simon & Pierre, 1990. 209-214.

New, W. H. *A History of Canadian Literature*. New York: New Amsterdam P, 1989.

Nothof, Anne. "Crossing Borders: Sharon Pollock's Revisitation of Canadian Frontiers." *Modern Drama* 38:4 (Winter 1995): 475-87.

Nunn, Robert C. "Performing Fact: Canadian Documentary Theatre." *Canadian Literature* 103 (Winter 1984): 51-62.

—. "Sharon Pollock's Plays: A Review Article." *Theatre History in Canada* 5:1 (Spring 1984): 72-83.

Page, Malcolm. "Sharon Pollock: Committed Playwright." *Canadian Drama. L'Art dramatique Canadien* 5 (Fall 1979): 104-06.

Parker, Brian. "Is There a Canadian Drama?" *The Canadian Imagination*. Ed. David Staines. Cambridge: Harvard UP, 1977.

Pollock, Sharon. *Walsh*. Vancouver: Talonbooks, 1974.

—. *The Komagata Maru Incident*. Toronto: Playwrights Canada, 1978.

—. *Blood Relations and Other Plays*. Edmonton: NeWest, 1981.

—. *Saucy Jack*. Winnipeg: Blizzard, 1994.

—. *Fair Liberty's Call*. Toronto: Coach House, 1995.

Rubin, Don. "Celebrating the Nation: History and the Canadian Theatre." *Canadian Theatre Review*, 34 (Spring 1982): 12-22.

Salter, Dennis. "(Im)possible Words: The Plays of Sharon Pollock." *The Sharon Pollock Papers: First Accession*. Comps. Sandra Mortensen and Shirley A. Onn. Eds. Apollonia Steele and Jean F. Tener. Calgary: U of Calgary P, 1989. xi-xxxv.

Turner, C. Frank. *Across the Medicine Line: The Epic Confrontation Between Sitting Bull and the North-West Mounted Police*. Toronto: McClelland & Stewart, 1973.

Vidyarthi, Ramesvara. *Komagata Maru ki samudra yatra* [The Sea Voyage of the Komagata Maru]. Mirajapura (Uttar Pradesh): Krantikari Prakasana, 1970.

Wallace, Robert, and Cynthia Zimmerman. *The Work: Conversations with English-Canadian Playwrights*.Toronto: Coach House, 1982.

Whittaker, Herbert. "Canadian West at Stratford." *Globe and Mail*, 22 July 1974.

Zimmerman, Cynthia. *Playwriting Women: Female Voices in English Canada*. Toronto: Simon & Pierre, 1994.

WOMEN AND MADNESS

SHARON POLLOCK'S PLAYS OF THE EARLY 1990S

Craig Stewart Walker

In a 1982 interview, Sharon Pollock speculated on the direction of her work to come, declaring:

> I think that the plays that I'll write in the future will be more about women. I know there's a play that follows *Blood Relations* about what happens to a woman who is unable to kill either her father or her mother or, indeed, even herself. Obviously it's about women and madness (*Work* 118).

Pollock's subsequent plays do indeed vaguely answer this description, exploring different configurations of "women and madness" in domestic, political, and psychological terms. In *Whiskey Six Cadenza* Leah feels helplessly trapped by her perverse relations with her foster parents (including Mama George's conniving at the situation), and ends up having Mr. Big kill her. In *Doc*, we see a daughter haunted by the spectre of her mother and grandmother's self-destruction, and by the overwhelming figure of her father: though in the end, the play embraces the possibility of positively reconciling parental-daughter tensions. But Pollock embraced the theme of "women and madness" even more directly in *Egg*, a play never produced in its original form, though from the large-cast *Egg* was eventually hatched the one-woman drama *Getting it Straight*. In *Fair Liberty's Call* madness is construed as the vision of a mother traumatized by war, and in *Saucy Jack* the madness and sanity are contingent upon the accuracy of memory.

The tone of *Egg* is quite unlike the work for which Pollock is best known. In some ways it resembles the kind of grotesque irony associated with George F. Walker. Among Pollock's works, it is closer to the absurdist satire characterizing her two early unpublished plays than any of the more subtle, psychologically-based drama she had been writing in the intervening years. However, *Egg* is far more complex and grotesque than either of those early plays. There are three interrelated spheres of action in *Egg*, arising from an attempt to show how multi-national corporations, military syndicates and ordinary human beings affect one another. The central character is Martha, an escaped mental patient who is the forerunner of Eme in *Getting it Straight*. It becomes apparent that Martha's "mental illness" is a result of her inability to live with the condition of the nuclear bomb threatened world created by patriarchal, corporate and militaristic interests. Her husband, George, is a general engaged in a promotional campaign intended, as he explains:

> to get people round the world behind the concept of war as a means to peace. There are worse things than turning the globe into a cinder falling through space, but it isn't an easy proposition to sell (24).

Consequently, when Martha escapes, the doctors decide not to "impose on the General at this time a lot of hullabaloo concerning a looney tunes wife he was basically warehousing at our institution" (24). Instead they announce that she is infected with a "deadly, eighteen-hour" virus.

Meanwhile, at the offices of Universal Inc., the military's partner in the "Whole Earth Nuclear" campaign, we see two contrasting groups. In one room, three women – a television producer, a financial officer and a secretary – unpack eggs from a carton and calmly discuss the problems of sexism in their homes. In another, the male CEO of the company, R.D. Farkerson, rants erratically and paranoically to a male subordinate about his distrust of the women who seem to be infesting his company:

> We are surrounded by women. Have you noticed that? They're everywhere. It's frightening. Everyplace you look. Women. I'm starting to notice their faces. I catch myself, every once in a while, looking right into their faces . . . We need some statistics on their numbers. Because I think there's more of them. And I'll tell you something else. There's got to be a reason the Chinese kept leaving them out on river banks because the Chinese are a very smart people (42).

As it turns out, Farkerson's fearful misogyny has some basis in the emergent circumstances for, led by Martha, a massive international coalition of women (and Beggs, the General's male assistant, who renounces his manhood and dons drag [51]) decides to overthrow the absurdly violent patriarchy and set up a peaceable matriarchal civilization in its place.

The approaching showdown between the male and female forces appears at times almost apocalyptic, though at others, a much smaller, localized revolt. Meanwhile, Martha rallies her followers with a series of strange inspirational speeches augmented with poetic passages from a disembodied "voice":

> MARTHA. We are living inside an egg, sisters, and the egg is blue, and if you screench up your eyes just a

little, open your mind just a little, and try to listen a little . . .
VOICE. . . . The unseen world is no longer a dream
It's floating just within grasp
A shimmering radiant heavenly orb
I know the way
To move, yes move towards that.
MARTHA. . . . We can stop the spread of war, we can give the word to the women of the world, that word's Unite. No more war. It's started, sisters. Listen. *(She holds the hand containing eggshells up. There is a murmuring of women's voices in a number of languages.)* All you have to do is believe, sisters. [. . .]
We take control. We talk to the world of women. We deliver a culture shock to the world of men via satellite link-up! We blast their dislocated minds into meaning.
We tell them loud and clear
We do not believe your promises!
We will not follow your commands! (50-52)

The women capture Farkerson and force-feed him a giant, boiled egg, including the shell. Farkerson regresses to a child-like state, and tells the story of how, at his birth, he was mistakenly named "R.D." by a nurse who did not understand that his mother was calling him "Artie" (60).

It appears that Pollock had not quite decided how to end the play when she abandoned it. The other men are still determined to fight, as they declare by singing:

> For fatherland, motherland, homeland
> We have the right to die
> We love our land, we'll make a stand
> Nation is all
> The state will not fall
> Let women wail
> Men will prevail (79).

But, as the forces outside besiege them, Martha speaks to Farkerson:

> Did you know, Arthur, that we are living inside an egg? And the egg is blue. It's a royal blue that's been lightened up with buttermilk . . . the egg opens up, like . . . a thousand suns . . . and the egg . . . says . . . stare ugliness in the face, don't . . . don't turn away from the pain and suffering . . . no . . . maybe you can just do a little bit . . . but if a great many do a little bit . . . then a lot will get done . . . (95).

And here the play ends, with a hint of personal responsibility, but with the plot largely unresolved.

Because *Egg* was never finished to a production-ready state (a note to director Guy Sprung makes it evident that this is an early draft), there are a number of outstanding questions which make it difficult to interpret the play with any great confidence. For example, it is tempting, with the hindsight bestowed by *Getting it Straight*, to consider the action as a projection from Martha's mind: a "psychomachia" drama. However, apart from the play beginning and ending with Martha's monologues, and a few non-realistic elements, there is not enough to support such a reading in the draft as it stands.

The non-realistic elements in the play would be at least equally compatible with the sort of fabulist, satiric propaganda which would be found in, say, Brecht's *Good Woman of Setzuan*. The puppets and songs and the montages of advertising and radio announcements which punctuate the action would neatly support an ongoing ironic commentary were that Pollock's intention; though as it stands the propaganda is rather underdeveloped.

At any rate, the political implications are better integrated in *Getting it Straight* (1989), the main difference being that everything is set unequivocally within the frame of a genuinely mentally distressed woman who is attempting to work out a sane understanding of an irrational world. Where, in *Egg*, the grotesque distortions sometimes detract from the political criticism, here the seamless transitions from legitimate fear and anger into paranoid terror and hostility not only make for a persuasive psychological portrait, but create a compelling, passionate argument for a sane and coherent world view.

In *Getting it Straight*, as Eme says at one point, "real and unreal [are] shuffled like a deck of cards" (89). That puts heavy demands upon the spectator or reader; but the difficulty of discriminating between sane analysis and insane distortion supports a main theme of the play, that sometimes insanity is the most rational response to a disordered world. Or, as Eme herself puts it, "they say I'm mad / I say enola gay little boy fat man!" (89). She is referring to the bomber plane, Enola Gay, and its cargo of atomic bombs which were dropped on Hiroshima and Nagasaki in 1945; "little boy" and "fat man" were the respective code names for the smaller and larger prototypes developed through the Manhattan Project.

The plot of *Getting it Straight* is fairly straightforward, though it takes some close attention to pick it out of the text. Eme (short for Emily), a mentally disturbed middle-aged woman, having been taken on an outing to a rodeo, has left her group and is hiding beneath the grandstand. Less clear is the background story to which Eme continually but elliptically alludes. Most of Eme's allusions are in the nature of personal memories of her immediate family. We hear, for example, of her affection for her grandfather, and also of minor, seemingly arbitrary details about her father and brother. It would be unwise to lightly dismiss any of these memories, however trivial they may appear, for perhaps the most important recurring theme in Pollock's work is that of memory besieged by social forces. For Pollock, the authentic recollection of the past is the chief means of establishing personal integrity, so most references to characters' personal memories are in some way crucial.

One passage, lifted almost verbatim from *Egg*, concerns Eme's father's name, transcribed at birth as "R.D.," rather than "Artie." The joke is not a rich one, so at first glance this seems an odd detail to preserve for transference from *Egg* into the new script. But, in a play dealing with mental illness, it is likely that Pollock is nudging our attention in the direction of history's most famous "R.D.," R.D. Laing. The idea is supported by Eme's mention of a "layman's guide to schizophrenia" (89): a reasonably accurate description of R.D. Laing's controversial, best-selling 1960 study of schizophrenia, *The Divided Self*. There Laing tried to invert established preconceptions about insanity by arguing that labeling some individuals as "crazy" is merely expedient mutual agreement used in dysfunctional circumstances where one person does not fit what has been determined to be the norm. Applied to Eme's situation, the theory implicitly asks whether it is not the "social norm" (which, during the Cold War, included the terrifying logic of maintaining nuclear overkill capacity to deter war) that should be regarded as insane. Thus, buried in the homonym "R.D./Artie" is the question: who is mad?

Another at first seemingly insignificant detail is Eme's recollection that, in childhood, the "only way bubu [i.e., her brother, now a wealthy and powerful man of forty-two] could win a board game was by divine intervention."

Her parents told her "games aren't that important let bubu win tonight" (101). This is a common parental request of an older sibling, but in context of Eme's anxieties about global power, it is a microcosm for passive acceptance of the geo-political "boys' game" of nuclear deterrence. More recent among Eme's scattered ruminations are her references to Myrna, apparently a fellow patient, and Freida, a patient who apparently jumped or fell to a concrete surface (107). It is difficult to tell whether this latter image is a fantasy or it actually occurred at the rodeo Eme has just fled, repelled by the violence inherent in the sport.

However, most striking among these ambiguous images are Eme's references to her husband's briefcase. To the extent to which these allusions can be made coherent, it seems she once secretly opened it, finding documents pertaining to nuclear warfare. She fears that, in a state of horror, she then murdered her husband (125). But this notion is dubious even to Eme:

> maybe I dreamt it
> myrna says they say I dreamt it
> I say no
> no
> I say strike out strike down this is a lesser
> crime I am guilty of that I accept that I hope I
> have killed him, to have known and done
> nothing? that is the crime of that I am not guilty
> not guilty of that (125-26).

Much as Laing questioned the validity of judgments about the madness of some people living in alienating and destructive circumstances, Eme questions the immorality of murder in a situation where to be peaceful is to connive at plans involving the possible obliteration of the human race.

Set against these "memories" is Eme's vision for the future, chiefly drawn from *Egg*. Indeed, Eme often uses egg imagery in passages taken almost verbatim from the earlier play:

> we are living
> inside an egg and I
> I see that it's blue
> and the egg opens up
> and a bright light
> like a thousand suns and if I can open my eyes
> just a little open my mind just a little try to
> listen a little [. . .]
> the visible world   is no longer real
> it's shattered   and turned into glass
> a mirror   of ugliness   agony   shame
> you know the way   you know the way to change
> to change all of that the unseen word
> is no longer a dream   it's   floating   just within
> grasp a   shimmering radiant   heavenly   orb you
> know the way to   move yes move . . . (123-4)

The egg image is appropriate in several ways: an egg encloses potential for future life, yet is sealed off from the outside world and the life within cannot emerge without effort; the fragility of an egg suggests the vulnerability of the earth, which can be destroyed through recklessness; the egg's surface is continuous, without beginning or end, like the vast unity Eme dreams of; the egg is associated with nurturing by females. As did Martha, Eme ends the play with a "call for action" to "all members of the female sex" (126). She envisions them spinning:

> ... a gossamer net of women's hand's and rapunzel's hair and that net will encircle the globe and if a person stood on the far left star of the utmost edge of cassiopeia's chair that net would twinkle in the inky cosmos like fairy lights on a christmas tree – and what would it spell? (126)

Earlier, when she recalls giving the same speech to Myrna, Eme's answer is "love." Myrna had laughed, so Eme furiously tried to smash Myrna's face into the floor (122). The irony of Eme's violent response perhaps indicates Pollock's scepticism, her awareness of the difficulties in realizing such a transfiguration of the world into a place of universal co-operation.

Still, Eme's interweaving of mythical figures and cosmic imagery to create a vision of universal harmony is undoubtedly pleasing. Her allusions to Cassiopeia (who aroused the wrath of the patriarchal Olympian, Poseidon, by boasting of her daughter's beauty), and to Rapunzel (locked away because of her beauty), raise again the question of whether it might not be that she has incurred entrapment because her thinking is too beautiful and good for the world, rather than too flawed. As usual, Pollock prefers the ambiguity of the open question to definite answers. Perhaps the biggest open question is inherent in the grandstand shadows cast across the space Eme occupies, suggesting, says Pollock in her opening stage directions, "what may be bars [or] ribs." Is Eme's condition necessarily one of imprisonment within the bars of insanity? Or is she, like Jonah within the ribs of the whale, trapped only temporarily in her despair, a stage in a journey whose ultimate objective is universal enlightenment?

With *Fair Liberty's Call,* Pollock returns to a historical setting comparable with the early history plays (in this case a 1785 Loyalist community in New Brunswick). *Fair Liberty's Call* also returns to the family-based themes she had explored in the 1980s. However, there are significant differences in the treatment of these circumstances in *Fair Liberty's Call*, which arise from the concerns Pollock had been addressing in the intervening years. For example, Joan, the matriarch of the Roberts family, is thematically related to Martha from *Egg* and Eme from *Getting it Straight*: a middle-aged woman who, through grief and despair, has become mentally disordered, unable to reason and often uncertain of her location or the identity of others. As we might expect from Pollock's previous work, Joan's mental state stands as a touchstone for the disordered world of the play as a whole. And, as we also may have expected, the environmental dysfunction here has something to do with unreconciled relations with the past. In this case, however, the dramatic issue is not focused upon one individual cultivating a healthy perspective on history; rather, it is the concern of a whole community. So Joan's predicament is much what we would see if we were to discover Eme, not secluded with her own thoughts beneath a grandstand, but among a fractious and confused family who had not yet foresworn the violent outlook which had caused her mental breakdown in the first place.

Joan's husband, George, is a former Bostonian loyalist who fought against the American Rebels, a violently-minded man who remains angry at the Rebels and embittered about being beholden in his adopted country to the plutocratic Committee of Fifty-five Families. Joan and George lost both their sons in the War of Independence, but they still have two daughters, Annie and Eddie. The latter was born Emily, but has been dressing and living as a man since she took her dead brother's name and place as a soldier at sixteen. An honourary member of the Roberts family is Daniel Wilson, Annie's fiancé and an ex-corporal in the loyalist Legion. The other two loyalist characters are Major Abijah Williams, representative of the local establishment, and Black Wullie, an ex-slave and scout for the Legion, and Eddie's loyal companion. Finally, there is Major John Anderson, who eventually reveals himself to be a vengeful Rebel.

All the characters are highly conscious of the need to establish correct relations with the past; but they are by no means in agreement about how these are to be constituted. The play begins with a series of interlaced speeches about the past. Pollock says of this scene:

> They have a compelling need to tell; to tell before someone else tells; to correct a former mistelling; to tell before they're unable to tell, or prevented from telling [17].

Despite this competitiveness to establish their own narratives, they are sensible of the need to arrive at some kind of joint account of the past. To this end, the loyalists of the Roberts household have devised a "Remembrance Ritual." "Totems, souvenirs and trophies of war" (36) are dragged out to invoke the honourable struggles that gave the Roberts family its essential identity. "Gotta fill the place up with things that speak of the past," says Daniel. To which the Major responds: "Else how's a man to know who he is" (37).

The impulse to affirm identity in this way appears to stem from a demand tacitly made by the land. The chorally shared first line of the play is: "You want to know where to put your eye so you can hear the heartbeat of the country comin' into bein'" (19-20). But by then Pollock has already introduced the idea in her description of the initial setting:

> A bare stage, the floor of which radiates in a dark-hued swirl of colour, represents the "virgin" land. Although this space appears empty and uncorrupted, it projects an aura of foreboding, a sense of the unseen. A subtle sound fills the space as if the air itself is vibrating just below the level of conscious hearing (19).

The sense of incipient power in the land effectively demands that the past be divulged truthfully, that the menacing emptiness of place be dispelled by the attention to the collective history.

As with all tribal recollections of primordial struggles, the problem is that there is a selective bias at work in the memories of the participants. An exchange between Annie and Anderson sums it up: "I notice you've got a powerful recollection of some things, and none at all for others." "An accident of war" (43). But even among supposed allies there is no guarantee of agreement. While the ritual is underway, the exasperated Major yells at Daniel, "You're not rememberin' right!" (53): that is, through the appropriate haze of veneration.

But the paramount source of dissent in the Remembrance Ritual arrives in the person of Major Anderson, the former Rebel who brings into this house his indictment of the Loyalists' merciless slaughter of the Rebels, including Anderson's fourteen-year-old brother, at the battle of Waxhaws. Anderson's plan is to hold the others hostage until the murderer of his brother is surrendered for execution.

In some respects, Anderson's function within *Sweet Liberty's Call* is similar to that of the Inspector in J.B.

Priestley's *An Inspector Calls*, or even the ghostly gunfighter in the Clint Eastwood western, *High Plains Drifter*: a stranger who, like an avenging angel heralding Judgement Day, arrives in an arrogant, corrupt and hypocritical environment to forcibly polarize differences and galvanize the search for truth among the inhabitants. Anderson's siege quickly shows that the pieties regularly invoked by the Loyalists throughout the play are hollow shams. The vaunted commitment to courage and honor crumbles into craven self-preservation as each man tries, by turns, to shift the blame onto the shoulders of another or to offer reasons why his personal value suggests that his life particularly should be spared. Or, more precisely: each of the white men reveals such despicable weakness. Pollock is careful to preserve the dignity of the one black man, Wullie, and Eddie, whose transvestism keeps her among the men (indeed, she proves the most "manful" of the lot).

What is behind Pollock's effort to discriminate between the behavior of those who are white men and those who are not is, I suggest, less a matter of insisting upon essentialist differences in race or sex than of her being interested in finding out fresh ground upon which less violent and adversarial cultural alternatives might take root. Surely a new world is conceivable in which people would see the incongruity in the very idea of a "due process" in condemning a man to death? And since those dominant in the established culture are male and white, the founders of Pollock's alternative culture are not.

In pursuing this optimistic notion of a new society, *Fair Liberty's Call* drifts closer at times to the conventions of romance than those associated with the history play. Reconciling these two genres poses no little difficulty. For where the ethic of the history play (at least in Pollock's hands) is founded upon the paramountcy of truthful remembrance, the ethic of romance is based in the hope of redemption, optimistic values having more to do with faith than with a ruthless scrutiny driving the search for historical truth. Where, after all, in examining the past, *does* one put one's "eye to hear the heartbeat of the country coming into being?" One is looking for "the substance of things hoped for, the evidence of things not seen" (cf. Hebrews 11:1).

Pollock's solution is to delicately juggle her depiction of the known facts of history so as to place them within conventions of romance that can accommodate real moral concerns. For example, taking her cue from the reciprocal moral transgression attached to both sides of the War of Independence, Pollock uses a version of the mirror-plotting common to many romances in order to lift the siege in this play. Anderson's single-minded determination to avenge his brother's death is dissolved when he finds himself faced with Annie's admission that she betrayed a Loyalist spy into the hands of the Rebels to avenge her own brother's death. Realistically, that this would suddenly end the hostility is no more "natural" than that the "natural perspective" embodied by Viola and Sebastian at the end of *Twelfth Night* should bring that play to a happy conclusion. Both devices are sleights of hand, using fortune's symmetries to distract our attention from the past, turning it to new beginnings. Thus, Major Williams becomes a sort of vanquished *alazon* figure, leaving the Roberts home with a final threatening speech like Malvolio's, thereby clearing the way for the inauguration of a new world. Joan, in a moment reminiscent of Hermione's resurrection and her reunion with her lost daughter, Perdita, begins to recover her life in the present, to see that Eddie is indeed her daughter, Emily. "It's a new world, Mama," says Eddie, "you gotta look up close" (78).

Finally, pursuing the hope for a better world Pollock hinted at when she preserved Eddie and Wullie from degradation, the freed slave and emancipated woman declare they will remain together to start a new family. Meanwhile, Joan envisages a blessing from another alternative to patriarchal authority:

> I feel my feet pressin' flat 'gainst the surface of the soil now. I kneel readin' the contours of the skull and listenin' to the words spoke by the man with the missin' jawbone, and the caps of my knees make a small indentation in the dirt. [. . .] And the red woman with the baby on her back steps out from under the glade of trees and she holds out a bowl, she offers a bowl of earth. [. . .] Eat, she says, swallow. And I do (79-80).

The new world being made here is meant to transcend the antinomies and violence of the old, to begin new lives, having acknowledged and atoned for the errors of history.

To be sure, Pollock could be charged with indulging in a biased mythologizing of the past not much different from that she condemns the loyalists for perpetuating, of succumbing to the temptation of wishfully revising the past by putting something as improbable as the Eddie's transvestism and union with Wullie into her play. But by this stage, Pollock had grown less interested in precisely reconstructing history than in exploring ways of reconciling her sense of the mistakes of the past with her project of encouraging ethical constructions for the future.

Pollock's recent play, *Saucy Jack* (1993), was certainly approached in such a frame of mind. *Saucy Jack* treats a subject that has fascinated many writers, the mystery of the most famous serial killer in history, Jack the Ripper. Yet, where most treatments of Jack the Ripper focus on the questions of who he was and why he committed the murders, Pollock argues that such questions are irrelevant. For her, the nub of the issue is that:

> the women are killed because they can be killed with relative or complete impunity. It is done because it can be done. That reason is sufficient for those who undertake such actions (*Saucy* 5).

To be sure, that may be a thin theory of human nature, and it disregards the obvious fact that the vast majority of the population living in London in 1888, notwithstanding opportunity, did *not* choose to become serial murderers and indeed were horrified by the crimes. After all, that is precisely why Jack the Ripper became so notorious. Still, the comment is a focused declaration of the political premises underlying this play. The character Kate might speak for Pollock when she sings, ostensibly as a warning to Montague:

> There's no time to tell you how
> He came to be a killer
> But you should know as time will tell
> That he's society's pillar
> For he is not a butcher
> Nor yet a foreign skipper
> He is your own light-hearted friend
> Yours truly, Jack the Ripper (28).

In short, social implications, not the personal details of the man known as Jack the Ripper, are the issue here. Accordingly, notwithstanding any similarities between *Saucy Jack* and Pollock's treatment of the late nineteenth-century's next most legendary murderer in *Blood Relations*, the differences are significant.

In *Saucy Jack* Pollock's political thesis demands that Jack should not be a lone, monstrous figure, but someone who operates with the assistance, or at least, the connivance, of others; the murders must not be seen as social transgressions but, on the contrary, as acts which enjoy social support. Hence, it is left unclear just who was responsible for the actual murders, Eddy (Prince Albert Victor, grandson to Queen Victoria and heir to the throne) or Jem (James Stephen, friend and former tutor to the Prince, and the more forceful personality). Responsibility is thereby spread, and a further blurring of the guilt will follow. Jem's plan is to displace suspicion for the murders onto their mutual acquaintance, Montague, by murdering him and planting evidence upon the body. However, the plan is not quite so straightforward as that, for he has also hired Kate, a "music hall entertainer and actor," to enact each of the murdered prostitutes.

Jem's motive for having the murders re-enacted is unclear, despite a comment of Pollock's which I will come to in a moment. In part, the uncertainty arises because Jem has received a head injury some time in the past which makes him frequently speak and behave in very peculiar ways. The play begins with a long, frighteningly irrational monologue which Jem delivers in the presence of Kate. Apart from its arousal of our anxiety for Kate's safety, the effect of the speech is to discourage us from expecting Jem's subsequent behavior to have logical reasons attached to it. Accordingly, while Jem says that his object in having the murders re-enacted is to "save Eddy," it is not at first apparent how this could be so, especially given that Jem is at least equally suspect. That element of sadistic nostalgia which prompts psychopaths to preserve souvenirs of their murders perhaps figures to some extent, yet this does not satisfy as a final explanation of Jem's motivation, because there is no sign of the salacious glee we would expect in such a case.

Pollock raises the issue in her introductory note:

> The end or objective or motivation for the re-enactment of the women's deaths in the play is not to achieve the death of the women, but to achieve some other end or objective that relates to the relationship between the men. Love, loyalty and friendship are words the men use, but the actions through which such noble sentiments manifest themselves are the ones of betrayal, duplicity and murder (5).

To be sure, they could hardly be out to "achieve the death of the women," because the women are already dead. Yet Pollock's point about the "objective that relates to the relationship between the men," remains cryptic. The men are indeed utterly despicable, but this is little help. In what sense does their discreditable partnership motivate the re-enactment? The point is clarified a little further on, when Pollock declares:

> I am less interested in whether Jem, or Eddy, or some combination of them and possibly others, are indeed guilty of the murders than I am interested in the whys and ways Jem attempts to bind Eddy to him as well as to confirm or negate his fearful suspicions regarding his own role in the Ripper events. He's caught in a terrible dilemma. If he is indeed guilty of the crimes, he is "sane" for his clouded recall is founded on reality. If he is innocent of the crimes, his memory and mind are serving up false data and he's "insane" (5-6).

Thus the key to sanity, in Pollock's formulation, is not whether one's *behaviour* is rational or psychotic, but whether one *remembers* accurately or not. This would be a rather remarkable assertion, were it not that we have been prepared for it by the decisive role played by memory in virtually all of Pollock's previous plays. Where Ibsen showed how the past could determine a character's destiny, Pollock shows how *retelling* the past determines one's destiny and, hence, sanity. Jem wants the murders re-enacted because he seeks validation for a certain version of the past. To be sure, at one level, he hopes Eddy can tell him who was actually responsible for the murders; but the main emphasis leans upon the issue of whether Jem and Eddy will remain partners in the act of recollection.

Further light is shed by the style of the re-enactments. It is quickly apparent that the vignettes are not meant to be realistic, either in the sense of capturing what the murdered women might have actually said in the street, or in the sense of being likely versions of what might be devised by two murderous aristocrats and a music hall performer. For one thing, the writing is too poetical to be commensurate with either such project. For example, Kate ends her speech as Polly in this way:

> Up and out and in, with the cry a slaughtered horses ringin' in me ears, and the press a Buck Row bricks markin' me back – But hold – look – look at the sky, it's glowin', yes it's . . . there's a wonderful fire down on the docks and it's lightin' up the heavens, oh I wish I could be there, see the flames feedin' on the wood, reachin' up over the water, the water and fire and wood, wish I could be up close, right in the middle, surrounded by flames burnin' in hell and floatin' to heaven on a spire a golden smoke (26).

Essentially, the speech is a stylized, poetic condensation of Polly's whole character, the combination of stream-of-consciousness, catch phrases, fragments of autobiography and mental imagery quickly, deftly adumbrating a whole life, a soul. The contrast between this and the coroner-like forensic inventory initiated by Jem which immediately follows could not be starker. For, in Kate's speeches, the important level of meaning lies not with mimetic but with symbolic and thematic concerns.

Plainly, then, the re-enactments in *Saucy Jack* have quite a different function from the re-enactment in *Blood Relations*, where the Actress enters into the terms of a reality prescribed by Miss Lizzie so as to work through the sense of Lizzie's situation, to sympathetically speculate on the motives for Lizzie's real or imagined behaviour. Miss Lizzie already knows what happened in the past; the re-enactment is intended to edify the Actress herself (and, of course, the audience).

The actress in *Saucy Jack* is far more autonomous. Because Jem does not himself know the extent of his and Eddy's role in the murders, he could not be much of a coach to Kate; and he certainly has no interest in teaching his actress. Indeed, it is pointedly established that the prior contact between Jem and Kate has been minimal (one is reminded of a magician's introduction of a "volunteer"). She is never called Kate by the others; her name and occupation may be known only to us. Except when performing, she remains a silent, anonymous figure, seeming to occupy a different level of reality from that of the men.

The significance of maintaining Kate's dramatic autonomy and of providing her with such evocative, stylistic renderings of the murdered women seems to be this: Kate is engaged in a sort of mortal competition with the men for the control of the past. The contest is mortal not in the sense that anyone's actual life is at stake (though Montague's is certainly endangered, and Kate's may be). Dramatically speaking, what is most potently at stake is the inner lives of the murdered women, and by inference, the inner lives of all women, their possession of their own souls. The matter is related to Pollock's recurrent theme of the role of memory in protecting individual integrity against deterministic forces. Jem seeks validation for his dubious memories even at the risk of conclusively establishing his own and Eddy's guilt. In Pollock's dramatic world, the power of recollection bestows not only sanity but validity; for those whose memories prevail set the terms of sanity, determining (cf. R.D. Laing) who is sane or insane, and thus, in essence, which truth claims are valid.

Hence, Jem passionately wants to "re ... member," as he frequently puts it, to reestablish the validity of his (and his class's) vision of the world by reassembling, or remembering, the dismembered fragments, as if with the dismemberment of the women's bodies there had occurred a fundamental disintegration of objective truth itself. But Pollock intends that Jem should find no such validation. Hence, far from re-establishing themselves as arbiters of truth, the men are made pathetic and impotent by their imperfect attempt to remember. In contrast, Kate grows stronger and more powerful through her vivid re-enactments of the souls of these murdered women.

Pollock writes that through her performances Kate evolves:

> ... from a silent, unknown, nameless figure [. . .] to the only vital or potent figure or force in the play when the final blackout occurs. Her exploitation has not victim-

> ized her; it has empowered her. She is larger than herself at the end. [. . .] She lives. They die (6).

It is irrelevant to object that Kate would not be allowed to escape with her life were the men really the ruthless murderers they are meant to be. Pollock has created a confrontation between two versions of the past to pose the question of which is more valid. And, because this trial unfolds within the dramatic imagination, the authority which determines the outcome of the confrontation is not that of social class, or brute force, or even political office, but an authority of the imagination that determines which is more convincing, which more compelling, which more truly vital. There is little doubt that, in such terms of the spirit, those like Jem and his cohorts are quite, quite dead.

WORKS CITED

Laing, R.D. *The Divided Self*. 1960. London: Penguin Books, 1965.
Pollock, Sharon. *Egg*. Typescript. University of Guelph Archives. n.d.
—. *Fair Liberty's Call*. Coach House Press: Toronto, 1995.
—. *Getting It Straight* in *Heroines: Three Plays*. Ed. Joyce Doolittle. Red Deer, Alta.: Red Deer College Press, 1992.
—. *"It's all make believe, isn't it?" – Marilyn Monroe* in *Instant Applause: 26 Very Short Complete Plays*. Winnipeg: Blizzard Publishing, 1994.
—. *The Making of Warriors*, in *Airborne: Radio Plays by Women*. Ed. Ann Jansen. Winnipeg: Blizzard Publishing, 1991.
—. *Saucy Jack*. Winnipeg: Blizzard Publishing, 1994.
—. *The Work: Conversations with English-Canadian Playwrights* (interview). Ed. Robert Wallace and Cynthia Zimmerman. Toronto: Coach House Press, 1982.

"Lookin' to a Better World for our Children"

The Concept of Inheritance in Pollock's Fair Liberty's Call

Kathy K.Y. Chung

This essay explores the concept of inheritance in Sharon Pollock's play *Fair Liberty's Call*. I am using the term "inheritance" in a broad sense to mean any property, quality, or immaterial possession received, taken, or derived from a former possessor (often but not necessarily an ancestor).[1] The idea of inheritance links the past with the present and gestures towards the future. Inheritance also involves issues of familial generations, hierarchy, power, identity, and complex questions of merit, choice, rights, and responsibilities. What is inherited can range from physical appearance and personality traits, to material possessions, occupation, information, name and social standing, to more abstract things such as rights, political promises and obligations, conceptual frameworks, moral values, and cultural identity. All these issues are germane to *Fair Liberty's Call* (as to many of Pollock's plays). For example, the Loyalists veterans gathered at the Roberts' home at the start of the play have inherited many things. These include guilt for the people they have killed in battle, the responsibility to remember the dead and to tell their stories (truthfully or not), the responsibility to each other as survivors and "brothers in arms" (whether they accept this responsibility or not). Equally, the "intruder" in the play, the Rebel Anderson, who demands a death, does so because he feels a responsibility to avenge his younger brother's death in the war. The question is, which of these "inheritances" will they honour, which will they reject, and why? Another form of inheritance involves the relationship between the political allegiances of George Roberts and of his children: George's coercive, paternal, Loyalist politics; Richard's decision to join the Rebels; Edward's decision to enlist in (and later to leave) the Loyalist legion; and Emily's decision to take over the identity of Edward/Eddie, her twin brother who had chosen to commit suicide rather than return to the inhumanity of war, and to carry on his military service. One may ask, what happens when the designated receiver does not wish to accept the "inheritance" or when the inheritance goes to the "wrong" person? Does the heir have a choice in the matter? These questions of free choice and familial responsibility are also central to *Fair Liberty's Call*.

Inheritance is an ambivalent concept. It can be conservative and limiting in its tendency towards solidarity, continuity, and repetition of former methods, structures, and values. Alternatively, the gift of inheritance can be liberating and enabling if it nurtures autonomy and permits difference (Bertaux-Wiame 40). In *Fair Liberty's Call*, the theme of inheritance, with its attendant imperatives of choice and responsibility, functions in expanding structures and relationships from the individual and the familial to the communal and the national. For the purposes of this essay, I will limit my focus to two forms of inheritance: the personal and familial, expressed in the form of property and identity; and the public and social, exemplified in two related areas: the linguistic, in terms of received languages; and the conceptual, in terms of ways of thinking and feeling, world views, logical structures. I caution that my taxonomy of forms is provisional, its boundaries dynamic, since each realm impinges on the other: language is a means of articulating and constructing conceptual structures and in Pollock's drama the personal and the social are inseparable. At issue here are questions of authority and choice: Can one choose to be a giver or receiver of an inheritance? Which inheritance does one honour? How does one arrive at one's decision?

I will argue that Pollock's ethics in relation to inheritance is weighted towards the present and the future. While there is a place for the reception and recognition of one's heritage, it is the freedom of choice and the responsibility to the future which Pollock emphasises. Though not as radical as the "Rebel" Thomas Jefferson, I think Pollock and her central characters Eddie, Joan, and Annie would agree, metaphorically, with Jefferson's 1789 proposition that, "the earth belongs [. . .] to the living" (qtd in Cunliffe 56) and no generation had the right to bind another nor dictate how its inheritance would be used (Cunliffe 56-57). Finally, I will point out that within *Fair Liberty's Call*, it is predominantly the women who seem most able to imagine alternative structures and choices, to transform themselves and their inheritances. One reason they are able to do this is that women were seldom seen by patriarchal society as legitimate inheritors of the dominant public discourses in the first place. They are more adept at envisioning a different perspective because their own lives attest to the existence of alternative, if devalued, experiences and world views.

"The World Upside Down": Familial Inheritance and Gender Reversal

> A family offer becomes a transmission between generations only when it is received as well as offered. And the form of what is passed down can be transformed in the transmission.
>
> Bertaux-Wiame 47

> JOAN. What happened to Em'ly?
> EDDIE. She's still here, Mama.
> JOAN. She's gone.
> EDDIE. She's changed.
>
> Pollock 78

As in "The World Upside Down," the song sung by the Loyalists during the revolutionary war, George Roberts' world has turned upside down. A former merchant and prominent citizen in Boston, he is, in the colony of New Brunswick, without occupation and social status. He states: "I remained true to the King and to Parliament, and I lost everything, and I end up here with nothin'!" (21). George's skill as a merchant does not seem in high demand in the new colony and, besides, the reality is that most of the wealth in colonial North America (and the colony of New Brunswick was no exception) was in the form of realty: land and buildings (Shammas 4). George tells Major Williams: "The only real money to be had in this country is land. You know it and I know it. Land is money and money's land" (32). However, to George's frustration, not only does he lack social and financial status in the male dominated public sphere, he is also deprived of his authority in the private sphere of the family. In the conventional order of things, land forms the bulk of the material inheritance passed on from generation to generation, it is what the father is able to bequeath to his family. In George's case, he must depend upon his son Eddie to acquire wealth and position for him:

> MAJOR. The greater part of the cash you'll see in a year is Eddie's half-pay captain's pension, and your largest allotment's his acreage for Loyalist Legion service [. . .]
> GEORGE. We're talkin' land allotment to members of the Fifty-five, and that's got nothin' to do with military service or rank.
> MAJOR. You forget, George. You're not a member of the Fifty-five (31-32).

George's reference to "the members of the Fifty-five" and their claim to land allotments despite their lack of military service or rank highlights another, negative, form of inheritance: the inheritance of power based on class rather than merit. Eddie's letter of political dissent in the *Gazette* (27-28) effectively anatomises and critiques the validity of this form of inheritance.

In addition to the lineal reversal, Pollock has also created a gender reversal. Eddie is not a man but a woman, Edward's twin sister. This truth, though hidden from the public, belies the social and gender hierarchies of patriarchal society and highlights the link between economic power, gender relations, and familial authority. In an attempt to assert his paternal authority, George insists:

> . . . Eddie is foolish and simple and easily led! (*The* Major *moves to replenish his rum.* George *follows him. Midway through* George's *speech,* Anderson *removes his hands from his pockets. He carries a recorder, and he begins to play "Revolutionary Tea.")* Eddie may give the appearance of a man, he may wield the gun and the sabre like a man, but Ed-

die needs guidance. Eddie will do whatever's required. For God's sake let's not leave it there (34).

The irony is that George is trapped by his own political and familial machinations. Since he has coerced Emily to replace Edward in Loyalist military service and since she fulfills society's expectations of the appearance and the actions of a man, he must now permit her the authority of a man. George cannot regain his masculine authority over his daughter by exposing her performance without jeopardising his own position. In any case, George is unable to convince the men that Eddie/Emily is either foolish, simple, or easily led. Certainly, her authorship of the letter in the *Gazette*, a fact of which the Major is aware and which Eddie is not afraid to acknowledge, speaks of a political consciousness and confidence the men in the play would hardly attribute to a woman in their society. Pollock's stage directions also reinforce George's powerlessness. The Major's movement during George's lines and George's need to follow him in order to retain his audience further demonstrates George's lack of authority.

Another thing which can be inherited in the family is identity: social, political, and personal. And this "inheritance" seems able to flow both ways with varying constraints and freedoms. In Jeffersonian terms, George Roberts has attempted to bind the next generation with his own "laws" and dictate how its inheritance will be used. Ultimately, he fails. Faced with the turmoil of political and social unrest and familial pressures to ensure the survival of their family, Edward and Emily choose to be only *temporary* inheritors of George's Loyalist politics while Richard, who joined the Rebels, refused that inheritance from the start. Later, even Edward and Eddie will choose to refuse their inheritance. In fact, perhaps symbolically, the twins end up making the same grim choice: in Eddie's words to George, "I was willin' to die for you then," "I'm not willin' to live for you now" (73). Interestingly, much as George would like to "dis-inherit" Richard, Major Williams's response demonstrates that he is unable to sever their familial connection:

> MAJOR. I was eloquent alright. The smell of bubblin' tar makes a man eloquent. What I lacked was a son in the Rebel army.
> GEORGE. I had no son with the Rebels! I cut that boy out of my heart (34).

It seems that some forms of familial inheritances can flow from the child to the parent and cannot be refused.

If refusal is not always possible, then, as Bertaux-Wiame proposed, perhaps the process of transmission can alter the form of the inheritance or perhaps the inheritance and the inheritor will change each other in a continuing reciprocal relationship. Eddie/Emily exemplifies this possibility. For the survival of the family, Emily agrees to take Edward's place, a transformation of gender identity. Once the choice is made, other transformations ensue. Eddie's new masculine identity gives her access to the patriarchal systems and discourses of authority and her experiences as soldier, settler, *and* woman, teach her to critique the masculine heritage she now possesses. The process has changed her and her politics. When the Major justifies the war by saying "There's some things have to be done and we had to do them," Eddie replies, "To stop and think then was to die, but now? Now I ask, what did we do it for?" (49). Later, when Eddie points out that she went to war for her father and her family, and George insists "It was the only way," she replies, "That's what you said" (73). Experience, an experience which tests received knowledge, has changed Eddie. Her father's words, articulating the old system of logic, can no longer sway her. While the inheritance George bestows is conservative, Pollock suggests that it is transformed in the transmission and the inheritance which Eddie will pass on in turn promises to be liberating.

The Instability of Our Inherited Discourses

> Instability is a quality inherent in language, just as it seems to be a condition of knowing and understanding; instability is part of our inheritance.
> Howells, "Instability" 157

One of the key ways ideology is transmitted is through language and language is one form of public, social inheritance. Pollock's Eddie critiques the dominant ideology by pointing to the instability of the language and political classifications of its chief agent, the Major. She exposes and throws into doubt the prescriptive and declarative power of conventional labels by offering counter terms which, seen from her alternative moral perspective, are more accurate. What the Major calls "incitement to rebellion" she calls "freedom of speech," what he euphemistically calls "indentured persons" she names "slaves," and when he asks her to "make available [. . .] information" she translates this to "inform" (33). His "rule of the mob" is, in her view, the rule of "the people" (48). Over and over again, Pollock dramatises and problematises the rigid application of terms and concepts like "Rebel" and "Loyalist" (45), "patriot," "traitor,"and "liberty" (25, 42), "equality" (64), and "due process" (69).

"LOOKIN' TO A BETTER WORLD FOR OUR CHILDREN" 159

Ultimately, what is being critiqued is the inflexibility of the dominant discourse and its speakers, their lack of mutuality, their inability to account for context.

Another way in which discourse as inheritance fails is represented by Joan's condition. She is, in part, a classic example of colonial alienation resultant from the gap between personal experience and the language available to describe it (Ashcroft 9). Her old vocabulary and categories prove inadequate. When Joan says, "One mornin' I found a feather on the doorstep," Annie corrects her: "We don't have a doorstep, Mama. We haven't had a doorstep since Boston. We may never have a doorstep again" (20). Joan continues: "And in the sky a bird was circlin'. A bird like no bird I know. The colours were wrong, and the size [...] this is a barren place. This wasn't home, isn't home, is no place I know, no, no place I know" (20). Without the language and its underlying conceptual schema to describe the flora and fauna of her new home, experiences either do not have conceptual value at all (the country, with its woods populated by the red woman and her baby, the bird, the bones of the Dead, is "a barren place") or they are "wrong," and it isn't "home." The "[p]eltin' rain" of her experience does not match the "soft rain" of her mother's world (71). Given this situation, what can Joan do to transform the barren place into home? Pollock's answer lies in Joan's relation to the other inhabitants of the land.

In one sense, Joan's cultural inheritance, the one she brings with her into the new colony, cannot function because there is already another inheritance in place, represented symbolically by the red woman (a mother like Joan) who watches her and the bones of the alien Dead she finds in the earth (20, 27). The response of patriarchal, white, British and European colonisers to the indigenous culture has, historically, been one of destruction and replacement: destroy the existing heritage, replace it with another. But in dramatising Joan's experience, I believe Pollock offers another possibility: what Howells calls "inheritance 'by adoption'" ("In Search" 58). At the very end of *Fair Liberty's Call*, Joan completes a story she has been telling throughout the play. The transformation of a complex set of imagery illustrates her changing subjectivity and relation to the environment. Where, before, her feet left no impression on the ground (27), now her knee caps leave a small indentation (79). Earlier, the skull she discovers in the woods *tells* her things (27); now, she *listens* to the words it speaks (79). Finally, she tells us: "the red woman with the baby on her back steps out from under the glade of trees and she holds out a bowl, she offers a bowl full of earth" (79) and "Eat, she says. Swallow. / And I do" (80). While Anne Nothof has pointed out the historical inaccuracy of this meeting (484) and while I can stand back and imagine a critique of this idealised scene in which the native welcomes and enables the colonising culture, I also recognise the enigmatic power of this symbolic narrative. One metaphoric interpretation may be that Pollock envisions a mutual relationship between the two women, the two mothers, a relationship in which the red woman offers a gift, an inheritance of sorts, and Joan receives the offer, assumes an inheritance by adoption, and is transformed in the process. Perhaps it is the sincere adoption, rather than the destruction, of the resident heritage which will truly transform the wilderness into home.

Imagining Alternative Choices

One can imagine Joan saying, like Atwood's Susanna Moodie, "I am a word / in a foreign language" (lines 19-20). But to be a word in a foreign language can be liberating as well as alienating. Inheritances can take the form of conceptual systems as well as material goods or social/cultural identities. To be able to speak a different language offers the possibility of articulating alternative logics, of imagining different choices and different outcomes. In terms of received knowledge and discourses, we are all, in one sense, inheritors. However, it is the defranchised members of society, alienated and oppressed by the dominant conceptual systems, who find it easier to question such an inheritance. From the very beginning of *Fair Liberty's Call*, Pollock gives us two examples of such a condition. While there is a significant difference in the degree of autonomy Black Wullie and Eddie possess, there is also a logical parallel between Wullie's description of the racist political and economic logic within which he is forced to function and Eddie's account of the treatment of Loyalist prisoners in the war. A Rebel-owned slave who fights on the side of the Loyalists (and can prove his Rebel ownership) will be freed by the Loyalists. A Loyalist-owned slave who does likewise will not be freed (21-22). An English-born Loyalist captured by the Rebels will be freed in a prisoner exchange. A colonial-born Loyalist taken prisoner by the Rebels will not be freed in a prisoner exchange because the English accepts the Rebel's claim that the colonial-born Loyalist is a traitor (27). Both stories illustrate a double standard in the prevailing ideology, a betrayal of trust, and a disregard of merit in favour of position and preferment.

While men like Wullie, Daniel, and Anderson can learn to see the mechanics of the prevailing ideology, it is the women who are able, consistently, to imagine a scope for change which the men, confident or hopeful inheritors of the dominant systems of knowledge, are unable to envision. For example, while Anderson recognises the existence of different "angle[s] of observation" (43), his remains trapped a conventional dualistic perspective. He demands a death for a death, unable to escape the closed circuit of "murder on murder, like the boots of a corpse makin' its rounds" (61). Seemingly the proponent of choice and responsible action, Anderson, like most of the men in the play, understands choice only within the conventional either/or structure of victim or victimizer, loss or gain, kill or be killed. Early in the play, Joan and Annie converse with Anderson about the war and the Loyalist Rangers with whom Anderson claimed he served:

> JOAN. Edward served with the Rangers.
> ANNIE. Edward hadn't the stomach for scalpin' so he left the Rangers, eh Mama?
> ANDERSON. If it's scalp or be scalped, you can't blame a man for scalpin', ma'am.
> ANNIE. Was that the choice? (37)

Annie recognises and challenges the limits of Anderson's logic. Though clothed in the language of cowardice (again, it depends on your angle of observation), Edward's action already suggests an alternative choice: to leave the battle field in an attempt to neither "scalp [n]or be scalped." Edward's subsequent suicide may be seen as the result of his inability to continue to extend the limits of his conceptional framework, to continue to imagine further choices. The women could not help Edward then, but they can help Anderson and the others "now." At the end of the play, in the midst of a conflict which seems to promise only more deaths, Annie converses again with Anderson:

> ANNIE. . . . And you could talk to me and laugh and call me Annie and kill me?
> ANDERSON. If I had to.
> ANNIE. Chose to. It's not them choosin', is it? It's you (71).

And Joan tells him, "Name yourself. Are you Richard or Edward? Are you someone I know?" (71). Finally, Annie asks: "Why don't you choose to ride out of here?" (71). A little later, Joan tells Anderson, "You can go now" (75) and waits. Miraculously, he leaves – without killing anyone. As before, Annie points out to Anderson that the logical constraints within which he operates are not absolute or deterministic: if he kills it is not because he "had to" but because he "[c]hose to." Joan's invitation to "[n]ame yourself" suggests the possibility of autonomous change, of difference. Finally, Annie and Joan offer Anderson a different logic, an alternative choice and an alternative responsibility: he "can go," step outside of the conception prison (note Joan's statement is not an order but an offer, the choice resides in Anderson), and he can choose to be responsible not to the child of the past, his dead brother, but to the children of the future.

"THE EARTH BELONGS . . . TO THE LIVING"

Ultimately, it seems to me, Pollock's response to the burden and the promise of inheritance is weighted towards the present, and even more heavily, towards the future. True, the inheritance of the past can be of value and merits recognition. Daniel says, "Gotta fill the place up with things that speak of the past," and the Major adds, "Else how's a man to know who he is" (37). In one sense, they are right. The past can be a form of context and context contributes to the construction of meaning and subjectivity. And there are responsibilities linked to the inheritance of the past, a responsibility to remember as fully and as honestly as best one can (for example, it isn't enough for the Loyalist veterans to remember only their victories or their heroism [52-53]) and, as Anderson's presence points out, a responsibility to acknowledge one's past actions. However, there is also a danger in the inheritance of the past. Bertaux-Wiame reminds us: inheritances can be conservative. The Major may be wrong. Perhaps the past can only speak of who one was, not who one is or will be. It is the present and the future which is open to change, in which choices can still be made. Anderson points out that his choice of Annie, "[a]n innocent," as his victim should the men refuse to choose another, would be "fitting and proper. Historically accurate." He adds, "I thought royalty lovers would appreciate that." Eddie's response is, "Don't talk about royalty, talk about the rightness of *now, this action right now*" (63, emphasis added). The word "now" recurs in the play, gaining force, demanding observance. For example, Eddie tells George: "I'm not willin' to live for you now" (73). Joan tells Anderson: "I can see you now" and "You can go now" (75).

And if the present is the time in which new choices can be, must be, imagined, then it is based upon the needs of the future that such choices are determined. Annie remembers and honors the dead but she tells Anderson:

> I know it [her betrayal of Major Andre] changes nothin' for Richard. Or Edward. Sweet Major Andre.

I wonder if he thought of me at the end . . . Sometimes I feel his name fillin' my head and pressin' hard on my lips to be spoke . . . There's nothin' I can do for him now. There's nothin' I can do to put paid to my brothers or you to put paid to yours. We oughta be lookin' to a better world for our children. That's the only way to serve our brothers (75).

It is the future generation which demands our responsibility and it is in building a better future that we best serve the past. The names of the dead demand to be spoken but Pollock, in *Fair Liberty's Call*, suggests that it is the inheritance we pass on, the inheritance yet to be created, rather than the one we receive which merits our attention now.

NOTES

1   The OED's definition for the verb "to inherit," includes "to take or receive (property, esp. real property, or a right, privilege, rank, or title) as the heir of the former possessor (usually an ancestor), at his decease; to get, or come into possession of, by legal descent or succession." It defines "inheritance" to include "any property, quality, or immaterial possession inherited from ancestors or previous generations."

2   In June 1783, fifty-five Loyalists in New York City who had been land owners and community leaders in various colonies petitioned for large land grants in New Brunswick. Though some of them may actually have served during the war, their petition was based on class rather than merit. They argued that the new colony would need an elite to lead the masses and they proposed themselves as that elite. Their petition failed after meeting strong opposition from the Loyalists citizens already in New Brunswick (Moore 143-44).

Works Cited

Ashcroft, Bill, Gareth Griffiths, and Helen Tiffin. *The Empire Writes Back. Theory and Practice in Post-Colonial Literatures.* London: Routledge, 1989, 1993.

Atwood, Margaret. "Disembarking at Quebec." *The Journals of Susanne Moodie.* Toronto: Oxford UP, 1970: 11.

Bertaux-Wiame, Isabelle. "The Pull of Family ties. Intergenerational Relationships and Life Paths." *Between Generations. Family Models, Myths, and Memories.* Ed. Daniel Bertaux and Paul Thompson. Oxford: Oxford UP, 1993. 39-50.

Cunliffe, Marcus. "'The Earth Belongs to the Living': Thomas Jefferson and the Limits of Inheritance." *Forms and Functions of History in American Literature: Essays in Honor of Ursula Brumm.* Ed. Winfried Fluck, Jürgen Peper, and Willi Paul Adams. Berlin: Erich Schmidt, 1981. 56-70.

Howells, Coral Ann. "In Search of Lost Mothers: Margaret Laurence's *The Diviners* and Elizabeth Jolley's *Miss Peabody's Inheritance.*" *Ariel: A Review of International English Literature* 19.1 (January 1988): 57-70.

—. "Inheritance and Instability: Audrey Thomas's Real Mothers." *RANAM Recherches Anglaises et Nord-Americaines.* XX (1987): 157-62.

Moore, Christopher. *The Loyalists. Revolution, Exile, Settlement.* Toronto: Macmillan-Gage, 1984.

Nothof, Anne. "Crossing Borders: Sharon Pollock's Revisitation of Canadian Frontiers." *Modern Drama* 38 (1995): 475-87.

Pollock, Sharon. *Fair Liberty's Call.* Toronto: Coach House, 1995.

Shammas, Carole, Marylynn Salmon, and Michel Dahlin. *Inheritance in America from Colonial Times to the Present.* New Brunswick, NJ: Rutgers UP, 1987.

Interview with Sharon Pollock

Anne F. Nothof

Nothof: What is your most popular play? The most often produced? Can you speculate why?

Pollock: *Blood Relations*. I think there's a couple of reasons. One is that it has good roles for women, and there are a lot of good women actors who have reached a certain age when there are not so many roles for them. I also think there's a crossover in terms of that: older women have played it, and younger women have played it. And the other thing is that it appeals to two kinds of audiences: the people who are into the intellectual or an ideological end of things get off on that part of it. The people who are just looking for a suspenseful murder-mystery kind of thing get off on that end of it, so I think it's cross-over in that regard. And the other thing, I think, in the best productions I've seen, and what really interests me in the piece both when I wrote it and now even more so, is playing with the nature of the assuming of role and the "observed" and the "observer," which is really the audience and the actor, and there's multiple levels of that. When productions are done that play with these levels consciously – it can't help but happen because the play is structured like that – we have an actor playing a role, playing Miss Lizzie who takes on two other roles – that of Bridget and that of an audience member, and each of those four roles that's she playing carries the other three with them. And then you have the audience who's watching all that, which opens up really interesting levels of meaning that resonate, part of which have to do with the nature of theatre, the nature of observing and reading meaning into watching somebody watch something. So I think that certain theatre people like it because they really get into digging into that end of it. I get letters from producers and directors saying that they had such fun with the play. Of course, there are other productions which just go off the surface (and it works that way). And why is Lizzie Borden still around? That's one of the reasons why it's popular. If I'd written about Laura Secord, it wouldn't have worked the same way.

Nothof: Is *Blood Relations* your favourite play?

Pollock: No, it isn't. I don't have a favourite play, actually. I think in some respects, I like *Whiskey Six*. I think it's a good play and it's interesting that nobody ever does it. It got the best overall reviews of any play I've written, a hot national press (the *Globe and Mail*). The University of Alberta Studio theatre production was wonderful – with an interesting set, and yet it never was picked up. But I think *Fair Liberty's Call* was an interesting piece too, and yet in this country it has no life at all. I do get the odd production mostly in universities in the States.

Nothof: So it hasn't been done since the Stratford production?

Pollock: No. And it doesn't have to be a costly production. People manage to take on Shakespeare – small companies – and cost isn't an issue at all. I believe that it is because it's a rich play, that television and film have devalued our artistic imagination . . . we're in a horrible artistic deficit. People don't want to dig into those things. You have to bring something to the party. You can't just show up. And we've got ourselves into this industrial mode of creation:

three and a half weeks whether you're doing *Salt Water Moon*, which you may or not need three and a half weeks to do, or *Fair Liberty's Call*, which you just can't do in that time. It's an art disciple. It's like saying to a painter, you have three and a half weeks to do every painting you want to do. It doesn't make sense. So the mode of creation mitigates against certain kinds of plays, not cost.

Nothof: The ensemble takes a while to bring together.

Pollock: And also how you choose how you are going to physically realize the first section of it – the prologue in which people speak directly to the audience. You need time to explore with the cast the different ways of doing that. The worst way is just to have them stand up and deliver.

Nothof: It must be extremely difficult to portray big chunks of history as you do.

Pollock: Particularly when nobody knows it.

Nothof: Your plays have been produced in many other countries. Have you seen any of these productions? In other languages?

Pollock: Yes, I've seen a Japanese production of *Blood Relations* in Tokyo, and that was wonderful. I've seen a number of them. I saw *The Komagata Maru Incident* in London, and it was done by a small company called "Jericho." It toured into all sorts of community centres. I saw it in a community centre in which I and one of the people on the stage were the only Caucasian people in the theatre. The audience was all Sikh. A black man played T.S., and I thought it was such a wonderful choice. I've always struggled with but never come up with a satisfactory answer as to why T.S. is telling this story. I've always said T.S. is telling the audience, "I will show you how we use you, and you will still come and watch and let that happen." But I've always thought that was an act of disrespect for the audience. But when a member of any marginalized group plays that part, it makes a difference. I've it done with a woman playing T.S. too. And when the Punjabi immigrants repel the ferry by throwing coal, and everybody in the audience started to yell "Jai Khalsa," along with the people on stage, it was quite fantastic. I've seen pictures of a production in India of *Generations*, and it was wonderful because someone had given a university there a batch of my plays and asked which one they wanted to do. There were a lot of farming families in the area and people who had some relationship to the land, and they chose *Generations*. I always think the plays will be transferred to the locale in which they are produced, but they aren't, at least the ones I've seen. And then I think, why am I surprised? We don't transfer plays into our locale either, or very rarely. And I've seen numerous productions of *Blood Relations*, mostly in the States and in Canada too, some of which have been fascinating.

Nothof: So your play was always recognizably Canadian?

Pollock: I've seen some productions away from Canada when the play has been deepened and enriched by what they are doing. But then I've seen productions in Canada in which somebody is making choices which open up the play in ways I hadn't thought of. And that's what you go for; otherwise it's so painful to see the play over and over again. I don't think "Canadian." I don't know what "Canadian" is. I think it's a term the government has created to administer us bureaucratically. I see the similarities with other countries, more than the differences. For example, I saw Australians as having an inability to penetrate beneath the surface of their country, and that made me think of us; in fact in *Fair Liberty's Call*, the mother talks about being unable to be rooted in that place, that there's a layer of bones that prevents her from growing in that place. Quite often the identification is with women in a production of *Blood Relations*, such as the director. Sometimes I feel more at home when I'm away, because we talk about theatre or politics, and often in Canada I feel isolated in my views on theatre and politics. Something in the work has spoken to them. I'm not sure what makes a work Canadian. At a Commonwealth conference in Germany, a Canadian academic denied that *Blood Relations* was "Canadian." When it was produced at the National Arts Centre, he felt that a cruise missile had detonated in Ottawa, destroying everything. I guess I should have written about Laura Secord and a cow. I can remember sitting in a university class in southern Ontario in which a student told me that *Walsh* was a regional play, that it couldn't be a Canadian play because it was set in the West. When you hear people tell you that your work is not Canadian, it's regional, you know that they wouldn't say that of Tennessee Williams. "Regional" is used as an adjective that defines and restricts. But also, in other counties, I may find myself on the opposite end of political viewpoints. But I don't believe that an artist should be a nationalist. I've written work that speaks to Canadians and I care about this place I live in. Its stories are my stories. And yet I refuse to allow that to define me in any way. What else could I be? Yet I share a distrust of the centre of power with the people in Oregon. Those are the connections I look at when I'm away – not the things that take me apart, but the things I'm the same as.

Nothof: What is your attitude to the play text – your own, or someone else's? To what extent can it be changed in production?

Pollock: It all comes down to what you want to change – your own or anyone else's. When I direct my own work, the actors tell me I don't respect the playwright enough. For me, the issue is what are we trying to communicate here? When you have an actor who finds it impossible to communicate with the music of a particular speech what needs to be communicated, and if by changing three words you can do that, with my own work, I'll change them quick as a wink. The same with stage directions. They reflect choices made at one time by one director. As a playwright you have to trust that creative, imaginative people are giving some thought to the play. There are things that shouldn't be changed, should never be changed. But for my own work, I've had people call to get permission to make changes in the dialogue for specific audiences, such as in a religious community or a high school situation. For a festival production of *Blood Relations*, for example, a teacher in Saskatchewan didn't have the women dance, and then apologized to me for it when an adjudicator criticized the omission. But there is a lot more in the play, so one omission, one layer gone, is not critical, although maybe the piece was diminished on one level. When you put a play out, you put it out for people to make their own. You hope they will do that because you trust that they know what the plays means. For example the "carousel" speech from *Blood Relations* is challenging to get right, and in my own productions, I have sometimes changed pronouns or verb tenses.

Nothof: Is the publication of your plays just one more step in the process?

Pollock: The publication of a play text is a record and a documentation of what worked for a group of people in a specific time and place. It's slightly more than a road map. But there may be many ways to do a show. What you want published is a text that will stimulate the creative imagination of theatre people who are going to produce it with their own vision of the possibilities of the work. But then there's the study of the work, where students require more text than what a theatre person does. Where a designer, or actor, or director does not require editorial instructions, a student trying to envision a performance does. The published version is your avenue to people who will read the play, and people who will produce it, and they need different things.

Nothof: What appealed to you about the Nell Shipman story – the subject of *Moving Pictures*?

Pollock: In the beginning I wasn't excited about the story. I didn't want to recast her to conform to our contemporary ideology. And she has the raw material in some aspects that makes it possible to do that with her, so she becomes this great forerunner out of her time. But I didn't really believe that was her. She had aspects of that, but if we really want to talk about her relationship with animals there were lots of aspects that were not forward looking at all. Even in her idea of film, we could explore differences between the "feminist" vision of a story and a "masculine" vision. But she never had any idea of the environment in which she worked. She never understood the economic environment of the studios and the place for the independent producers. She wasn't someone who rejected the system to do it her way; she was more someone who did it her way, and couldn't understand why it wasn't working better. She wasn't particularly perceptive. In the beginning that was a real blocking point for me. I wasn't interested in writing a documentary. I wanted to find a way into this woman that provides a doorway to us. I was less interested in finding a doorway into her. After doing a lot of research, and beginning to create out of the raw material a rough idea, and to discard material, and I found that Nell becomes her own person, and gradually I became engaged in the reasons for telling stories in general. My basic idea was that of an older woman telling her story, at the end of her life saying that it didn't mean anything, and wondering what she lived for. In the retelling of those other elements of her, two different characters carry the weight of two other aspects of self. She experiences her life by telling stories about her life that living her life never gave her. Meaning is derived from the act of telling the story. Meaning is not derived from living the story. And then to have that idea of the man who is the creator of the medium she works in – how his definition of the medium is applied to her own life: "the illusion of continuous movement through persistence of vision." If she takes that, it becomes the definition of her own failure.

Nothof: Your current project is also for Theatre Junction, for the 1999-2000 season – entitled *End Dream*. The story, which is about the murder of a white woman, and the Chinese man who was accused but acquitted, was dramatized a couple of years ago – entitled *Disposing of the Dead* by Kate Schlemmer, produced by Pink Ink and Axis Theatre at the Waterfront Theatre, and directed by Sandhano Schultze. Did you see this play?

Pollock: No, but I did see a very good videotape of the play. I stopped working on *End Dream*, but then realized that for *Disposing of the Dead* the story was a hook to hang an imagistic theatre experience from, an avenue to do interesting things with sound and sight. I ended up feeling that mine would be sufficiently different, and so I went back to working on it. I have another piece, which is about Eugene O'Neill and Zelda. It was a terrible thing when she was locked up in an institution in which the psychiatrist and Eugene forced her to sign a piece of paper that gave away the rights to her life both before meeting him and after living with him to Scott Fitzgerald for material for his books. I'm fascinated by Zelda and how she became what they wanted her to be. There's a lot of "medicalizing" of her lately, attempting to account for her behaviour. But what happened first? Was she not happy being a mother because of a "chemical imbalance"? I don't think so. At some point you have to talk about the things she's saying, and what she's feeling. When you're able to define them as "illness" it makes them illegitimate statements, when in fact they were perfectly legitimate statements. And after a while, she attributed those statements to being ill, so whenever she was unhappy with what they assigned her to do, she herself began to say, "Now I'm sick. I have to go away and get my head rearranged."

Nothof: You have been very much involved in teaching playwriting, and in workshopping plays. Do you use any particular strategies in new play development?

Pollock: I work as a director. I think a good director is good a dramaturge. I don't like dramaturgy on its own. We see dramaturgy as a way for young directors to get into directing. It becomes an avenue. The relationship between the playwright and the director is the right relationship. I'm looking for the meaning of the text, how it all hangs together. But the play only lives in performance, so you have to consider the physical realization of the text – what people are able to play and what they aren't able to play. I think of myself when I'm working with a playwright as opening up choices. The power is always with the playwright. I actually think the workshop process doesn't serve plays very well. It serves plays based on psychological examination of characters, and that's why so much anglophone Canadian theatre is so boring. Sitting around a table talking about stuff makes it not even literary; it makes it TV. It makes it superficial and shallow, and everything gets explained and answered, and the most interesting things are those that can't be explained and answered. Answering is putting everything in a box and limiting it. Why does Hedda Gabler shoot herself?

Nothof: Do you feel that a playwright should have theatre experience in order to write well for the theatre?

Pollock: It certainly helps. I also know that there are playwrights who have a sense of the dramatic and the theatre, but they may hate going to the theatre. That's something you can't give anybody. And then there are people who write very "crafty" plays, that are "adequate," and in fact a lot of them get produced. But there is no passion, no voice, no soul. There's tons of craft, from an intelligent, educated person, who has worked in the theatre and knows what works – a "craftsman." You never know where a wonderful playwright or play is going to come from. You just have to be open to that. "Craft" is the one thing you can help somebody with.

Nothof: You have also directed many plays, including your own. Do you enjoy directing your own plays?

Pollock: Yes, I do. I learn a lot more about them by directing them. When you're directing your own work, you don't have to consult with the playwright. The playwright is already there.

Nothof: Have you directed a play where the playwright is present?

Pollock: Yes. I've done workshop presentations with playwrights who are very inexperienced. And that's different, because a playwright with experience gives you a lot more leeway. They understand that the director has a certain vision too. It may an interpretive vision, but the director must have creative freedom too. You begin with respect and believing that we are all rational people, and so you hope that as a rational person you can explain to somebody why it is that cutting pages would be an asset. If you can't make your case, then you can't do it.

Nothof: How important to your work is it to have your own theatre space?

Pollock: One of the terrible things for playwrights is that they never get inside theatres unless their plays are being produced, which is sometimes not a very good time to be there.

Nothof: Do you think it an ideal situation for a playwright to have a connection with a specific theatre for which to write?

Pollock: I don't believe that is the case when the end result is that it closes off opportunities for other playwrights. And so, somehow, what you want is to work with people that you know and respect. When it becomes another way of exclusion for other playwrights, then I'm uneasy with that. You need new blood, new insight, new places to go.

Nothof: How important was the Garry Theatre project to your work as a playwright and director?

Pollock: My own plays were part of the whole scene. The Garry Theatre grew out of my belief in breaking down the artificial distinctions between professional theatre and community theatre. Theatre should be rooted in a community, and grow in a community, not a hot-house product from somewhere else. It was my small way of trying to put it in a people place, to accommodate a mix of people at various stages in the theatre, recognizing that some people have a great commitment to the theatre, and but who can't do only that.

Nothof: Do you see this community connection happening in other countries or societies?

Pollock: There's much more of a crossover in developing societies, at festivals where a company of actors work at other jobs, and do this too. We have community theatre here too, but it doesn't get covered in the press, which tends to demean it. However, if a group is ideologically based, then it gets some coverage and recognition.

Nothof: Was your experience at Stratford a good way to reach an audience?

Pollock: For *Walsh* we had a company that just did that show, not part of the major company. *One Tiger to a Hill* and *Fair Liberty's Call* were done by people who were also part of the major company – playing other roles in Shakespeare etc. Out of an eight week rehearsal period there were three weeks total of interspersed rehearsal. I had wonderful actors and directors, but the process does not serve new work well.

Nothof: You have been pessimistic about the state of Canadian theatre in the past. Do you still feel this way?

Pollock: If I look at the flagship theatre in my community, I don't see an exciting and interesting season. Regional theatres are still doing few new Canadian plays. In the interests of economy, the choices have become homogenized.

Nothof: Is there a limit to what can be staged? Are there subjects which you wouldn't tackle?

Pollock: The power of metaphor and a shared cultural literacy make almost anything possible. It is important to reach beyond special interests that address specific audiences – whether they be feminist, gay, or "survivor" audiences – to things which govern many people's lives. *Death of a Salesman* is not just about a salesman. The final act of violence in *Buried Child* is effected through a metaphor that is more horrific than a physical enactment of rape. Theatre is at its most powerful when it is least literal.

Alberta Playwrights' Network, Calgary,
May 22, 1999

Biography of Sharon Pollock

Sharon Pollock was born in 1936 in Fredericton, New Brunswick, the daughter of physician and MLA, Everett Chalmers, on whom the portrait of "Doc" in the play by that name is based. She attended the University of New Brunswick, but left before graduating in 1954 to marry Ross Pollock, a Toronto insurance broker. When they separated in the early 1960s, she returned to Fredericton with her five children. She worked at the Playhouse Theatre in Fredericton at various jobs, including some acting, then moved to Calgary in 1966 with actor Michael Ball. She toured with the Prairie Players in 1966, and won a Dominion Drama Festival award for her performance in Ann Jellico's *The Knack*. She began writing her first play, *A Compulsory Option*, while expecting her sixth child; this unpublished play won an Alberta Culture playwriting competition in 1971, and premiered in 1972 at the New Play Centre in Vancouver. *Walsh* premiered at Theatre Calgary in 1973, and the following year it was produced at the Stratford Festival in the Third Stage theatre. While living in Vancouver, she wrote children's plays for Playhouse Holiday and Playhouse Theatre School, and radio plays for the CBC. *And Out Goes You?* was first produced at the Vancouver Playhouse in 1975, and *The Komagata Maru Incident* at the same theatre the following year. Pollock played Lizzie in her next play, *My Name Is Lisbeth*, when it was produced at Douglas College, Surrey, B.C. in 1976. The same year, she worked at the University of Alberta as a playwriting instructor.

Pollock returned to Calgary in 1988. It has become for her an emotional as well as a physical home base: she maintains that "you don't always come from the place you're born in. The trick is to recognize it" (quoted in O'Grady). In 1999 she was awarded the Harry and Martha Cohen award for her significant contribution to Calgary theatre. *One Tiger to a Hill* premiered in Edmonton in 1980 at the Citadel Theatre; *Blood Relations* at Edmonton's Theatre 3, *Generations* at Alberta Theatre Projects, Calgary in 1980; *Whiskey Six Cadenza* in 1983, and *Doc* at Theatre Calgary in 1984. She has been artistic director at both Theatre Calgary (1984) and Theatre New Brunswick (1988), her tenure at both theatres cut short by differences of opinion over artistic direction with the board. She has also been playwright in residence at Alberta Theatre Projects and the National Arts Centre, and head of the playwrights' colony at the Banff Centre for the Arts (1977-80). In 1981 she returned to performing, as Miss Lizzie in Theatre Calgary's production of *Blood Relations*, and in her monologue, *Getting it Straight* (1989), at the International Women's Festival in Winnipeg, and at the Fringe Theatre Festival in Edmonton.

In 1993 *Fair Liberty's Call* premiered at the Stratford Festival and *Saucy Jack* opened at the Garry Theatre in Calgary under her direction. *Moving Pictures* opened in 1999, and *End Dream* in 2000, both at Theatre Junction in Calgary.

Sharon Pollock has received many awards for her plays: the Governor General's Award for *Blood Relations* in 1981 and *Doc*, the Canada Australian Literary Award in 1987, a Japan Foundation Award in 1995, the Nellie Drama Award for her radio play, *Sweet Land of Liberty* (1981), and a Golden Sheaf Award for her writing for television.

In 1998, she was elected president of the Alberta Playwrights Network. She continues to encourage new writing and new playwrights, and remains committed to the life of the theatre.

Works Cited

O'Grady (Nothof), Anne. "Sharon Pollock: Theatre Relationships," *The Athabasca University Magazine* 8.3 (Winter 1983/84): 21-23.

Bibliography

Published Stage Plays

Pollock, Sharon. "Blood Relations." *Canadian Theatre Review,* 29 (Winter 1981): 46-97.

Pollock, Sharon. "Blood Relations." *Plays By Women,* Vol. 3, ed. Michelene Wandor. London; New York: Methuen, 1982: 91-122.

Pollock, Sharon. *Blood Relations and Other Plays,* eds. Diane Bessai and Don Kerr. Edmonton: NeWest Press, 1981.

Pollock, Sharon. *Doc.* Toronto: Playwrights Canada, 1986, c1984.

Pollock, Sharon. "Doc." *Modern Canadian Plays,* ed. Jerry Wasserman. 3rd ed. Vancouver: Talonbooks, 1994: 129-167.

Pollock, Sharon. *Fair Liberty's Call.* Toronto: Coach House Press, 1995.

Pollock, Sharon. "Getting it Straight." *Heroines: Three Plays,* ed. Joyce Doolittle. Red Deer: Red Deer College Press, 1992.

Pollock, Sharon. "'It's All Make-Believe, Isn't It?'– Marilyn Monroe." *Instant Applause: 26 Very Short Complete Plays.* Winnipeg: Blizzard, 1994.

Pollock, Sharon. *The Komagata Maru Incident.* Toronto: Playwrights Co-op, 1978.

Pollock, Sharon. "The Komagata Maru Incident." *Six Canadian Plays,* ed. Tony Hamill. Toronto: Playwrights Canada Press, 1992.

Pollock, Sharon. "Prairie Dragons." *Playhouse: Six Fantasy Plays For Children,* ed. Joyce Doolittle. Red Deer: Red Deer College Press, 1989.

Pollock, Sharon. *Saucy Jack.* Winnipeg: Blizzard, 1994.

Pollock, Sharon. *Walsh.* Vancouver: Talonbooks, 1973.

Pollock, Sharon. "Walsh." *Modern Canadian Plays,* ed. Jerry Wasserman. 3rd ed. Vancouver: Talonbooks, 1993: 237-271.

Pollock, Sharon. "Whiskey Six Cadenza." *NeWest Plays By Women,* eds. Diane Bessai and Don Kerr. Edmonton: NeWest Press, 1987: 137-247.

Unpublished Stage Plays

Pollock, Sharon. *And Out Goes You?* Vancouver: Vancouver Playhouse, 1975.

Pollock, Sharon. *Chautaqua Spelt E-N-E-R-G-Y*. Calgary: Alberta Theatre Projects, 1979.

Pollock, Sharon. *A Compulsory Option*. Vancouver: New Play Centre, 1972.

Pollock, Sharon. *The Great Drag Race or Smoked, Choked and Croaked*. MS., Commissioned by the Christmas Seal Society of British Columbia, 1974.

Pollock, Sharon. *The Happy Prince*. Adaptation of the Oscar Wilde Story. Vancouver: Playhouse Theatre School, 1974.

Pollock, Sharon. *Hon/Harold*. MS., 1972.

Pollock, Sharon. *Lesson in Swizzlery*. New Westminster: Caravan, 1974.

Pollock, Sharon. *Mail vs. Female*. Calgary: Lunchbox Theatre, 1979.

Pollock, Sharon. *Mother Love*. MS., 1972.

Pollock, Sharon. *Moving Pictures*. Calgary: Theatre Junction, 1999.

Pollock, Sharon. *My Name Is Lisbeth*. Vancouver: Douglas College, 1976; rewritten as *Blood Relations*.

Pollock, Sharon. *New Canadians*. Vancouver: Playhouse Holiday, 1973.

Pollock, Sharon. *The Rose and the Nightingale*. Adaptation of the Oscar Wilde Story. Vancouver: Playhouse Theatre School, 1974.

Pollock, Sharon. *Star Child*. Adaptation of the Oscar Wilde Story. Vancouver: Playhouse Theatre School, 1974.

Pollock, Sharon. *Superstition Throu' the Ages*. Vancouver: Playhouse Holiday, 1973.

Pollock, Sharon. *Tracings: The Fraser Story*. Edmonton: Theatre Network, 1977.

Pollock, Sharon. *Untitled Libretto*. MS., Commissioned by Banff Centre of the Arts, 1978-1980.

Pollock, Sharon. *Wedjesay?* Vancouver: Playhouse Holiday, 1974.

Pollock, Sharon. *The Wreck on the National Line Car*. Calgary: Alberta Theatre Projects, 1978.

RADIO AND TELEVISION WRITING

Pollock, Sharon. "The Making of Warriors." *Airborne: Radio Plays by Women*, ed. Ann Jansen. Winnipeg: Blizzard, 1991.

Pollock, Sharon. *31 for 2*. TS. CBC Radio, 1971.

Pollock, Sharon. *The B Triple P Plan*. TS. CBC Radio, 1972.

Pollock, Sharon. *Country Joy*. Six 30-minute scripts. TS. CBC Television, 1978.
Pollock, Sharon. *Generation*. TS. CBC Radio, 1979.
Pollock, Sharon. *In Memory Of*. TS. CBC Radio, 1975.
Pollock, Sharon. *Intensive Care*. TS. CBC Radio, June 1983.
Pollock, Sharon. *The Komagata Maru Story*. TS. CBC Radio, 1976.
Pollock, Sharon. *The Larsens*. TS. CBC Television, 1974.
Pollock, Sharon. *Mary Beth Goes to Calgary*. TS. CBC Radio, 1980.
Pollock, Sharon. *Mrs. Yale and Jennifer*. Eight Episodes. TS. CBC Radio, 1980.
Pollock, Sharon. *The Person's Case*. TS. Access Television, 1979; first appeared under the working title, *Free Our Sisters, Free Ourselves*.
Pollock, Sharon. *Portait of a Pig*. TS. CBC Television, 1974.
Pollock, Sharon. *Ransom*. TS. CBC Television, 1976.
Pollock, Sharon. *Split Seconds in the Death Of*. TS. CBC Radio, 1971.
Pollock, Sharon. *Sweet Land of Liberty*. TS. CBC Radio, 1981.
Pollock, Sharon. *Waiting*. TS. CBC Radio, 1973.
Pollock, Sharon. *We to the Gods*. TS. CBC Radio, 1972.

CRITICAL ARTICLES AND INTERVIEWS

Agnew, Theresa. *Let Her But Breathe: Changing Representations of Women in Plays by Prairie Women Playwrights*, MA Thesis. Edmonton: University of Alberta, 1994.

Balcon, D. "A Question of Copyright: The Sharon Pollock Case." *Cinema Canada*, 102 (December 1983): 26-27.

Bessai, Diane. "Introduction." *Blood Relations and Other Plays*. Edmonton: NeWest Press, 1981: 7-9.

Bessai, Diane. "Sharon Pollock's Women: A Study in Dramatic Process." *A Mazing Space: Writing Canadian Women Writing*, eds. Shirley Neuman and Smaro Kamboureli. Edmonton: Longspoon/NeWest Press, 1986: 126-136.

Bessai, Diane. "Women Dramatists: Sharon Pollock and Judith Thompson." *Post-Colonial English Drama: Commonwealth Drama Since 1960*, ed. Bruce King. London: Macmillan, 1992: 97-117.

Clement, Susan, and Esther Beth Sullivan. "The Split Subject of *Blood Relations*." *Upstaging Big Daddy: Directing Theatre as if Gender and Race Matter*, eds. Ellen Donkin and Susan Clement. Ann Arbor: University of Michigan Press, 1993: 53-66.

Conolly, L.W., ed. *Canadian Drama and the Critics*. Vancouver: Talonbooks, 1987: 134-135, 259-276.

Dufort, Lynn. "Sharon Pollock Talks About Her New Work." *Foothills*, 2.2 (1986): 3-5.

Dunn, Margo. "Sharon Pollock: In the Centre Ring." *Makara*, 1.5 (August-September 1976): 2-6.

Gilbert, Reid. "'My Mother Wants Me To Play Romeo Before It's Too Late': Framing Gender On Stage." *Theatre Research in Canada/Recherches Théâtrales au Canada*, 14.2 (1993): 123-143.

Gilbert, Reid. "Sharon Pollock." *Profiles in Canadian Literature 6*, ed. Jeffrey M. Heath. Toronto: Dundurn, 1986: 113-120.

Gilbert, S.R. "Sharon Pollock." *Contemporary Dramatists*, ed. James Vinson. 3rd ed. London: Macmillan, 1982: 642-645.

Hayes, Christopher. "Miss Pollock Downs Her Axe. She Settles Out of Court: The Borden Film Goes On." *Alberta Report*, 10 (June 20, 1983): 45.

Hayes, Christopher. "Miss Pollock Gives CFCN 40 Whacks: The Court Freezes the TV Adaptation of Her Lizzie Borden Play." *Alberta Report*, 10 (May 16, 1983): 38.

Hofsess, John. "Families." *Homemaker's Magazine*, 15 (March 1980): 41-60.

Hofsess, John. "Sharon Pollock Off-Broadway: Success as a Subtle Form of Failure." *Books in Canada*, 12 (April 1983): 3-4.

Hohtanz, Marie. "Passionate Playwright." *Calgary Herald Sunday Magazine*, 29 November 1987: 6-10.

Hustak, Alan. "A Very Dramatic Exit: Playwright Pollock Quits Theatre Calgary." *Alberta Report*, 11 (September 10, 1984): 40-41.

Ingram, Anne. "Right Theatre at the Right Time: Sharon Pollock Takes New Brunswick by Storm." *Performing Arts*, 24 (July 1988): 12-13.

Jansen, Ann. "Change the Story: Narrative Strategies in Two Radio Plays." *Contemporary Issues in Canadian Drama*, ed. Per Brask. Winnipeg: Blizzard, 1995: 86-102.

Kerr, Rosalind. "Borderline Crossings in Sharon Pollock's Out-law Genres." *Theatre Research in Canada*, 17.2 (1996): 200-215.

Knelman, Martin. "Daddy Dearest: Sharon Pollock's *Doc*." *Saturday Night*, 99 (October 1984): 73-74.

Knowles, Richard Paul. "Replaying History: Canadian Historiographic Metadrama." *Dalhousie Review*, 67 (1987): 228-243.

Loiselle, André. "Paradigms of 1980s Québécois and Canadian Drama: Normand Chaurette's *Provincetown Playhouse, juillet*

1919, j'avais dix-neuf ans and Sharon Pollock's *Blood Relations*." *Quebec Studies*, 14 (Spring/Summer 1992): 93-104.

Loucks, Randee. *Sharon Pollock: 1973-1985. Playwright of Conscience and Consequence*, Unpublished MA Thesis. Calgary: University of Calgary, 1985.

McKinley, Marilyn. "Sharon Pollock's Bloody Relations: A TV Adaptation of Her Hit Play Enrages the Calgary Writer." *Alberta Report*, 10 (February 28, 1983): 36.

Messenger, Ann P. "More Utile than Dulce." *Canadian Literature*, 65 (Summer 1976): 90-95.

Metcalfe, Robin. "Interview with Sharon Pollock." *Books in Canada*, 16 (March 1987): 39-40.

Miner, Madonna. "'Lizzie Borden Took an Ax': Enacting *Blood Relations*." *Literature in Performance*, 6 (April 1986): 10-21.

Much, Rita, ed. "Reflections of a Female Artistic Director." *Women on the Canadian Stage*. Winnipeg: Blizzard, 1992: 109-114.

Much, Rita. "Theatre by Default: Sharon Pollock's Garry Theatre." *Canadian Theatre Review*, 82 (Spring 1995): 19-22.

Mullaly, Edward, J. "The Return of the Native." *Canadian Theatre Review*, 63 (Summer 1990): 20-24.

Nothof, Anne. "Crossing Borders: Sharon Pollock's Revisitation of Canadian Frontiers." *Modern Drama*, 38 (Winter 1995): 475-487.

Nothof, Anne. "Gendered Landscapes: Synergism of Place and Person in Canadian Prairie Drama." *Great Plains Quarterly*, 18.2 (Spring 1998): 127-138.

Nunn, Robert C. "Sharon Pollock's Plays: A Review Article." *Theatre History in Canada*, 5.1 (Spring 1984): 72-83.

Page, Malcolm. "Sharon Pollock: Committed Playwright." *Canadian Drama*, 5.2 (Fall 1979): 104-111.

Perkyns, Richard. "Generations: An Introduction." *Major Plays of the Canadian Theatre, 1934-1984*. Toronto: Irwin, 1984: 605-608.

Plant, Richard. "Precious Blood." *Books in Canada*, 11 (April 1982): 8-12.

Pollock, Sharon. *Canadian Literature*. Toronto: CMEC; Calgary: Access Network, c1984; videorecording.

Pollock, Sharon. "Dead or Alive: Feeling the Pulse of Canadian Theatre." *Theatrum*, 23 (April/May 1991): 12-13.

Rempel, Byron. "Not a Diplomat, Pollock Returns Dismayed at Canadian Theatre." *Alberta Report*, 16 (November 6, 1989): 56-57.

Rudakoff, Judith, and Rita Much, eds. *Fair Play*. Toronto: Simon & Pierre, 1990: 208-220.

Russell, David. *The Direction of Whiskey Six*, Unpublished MFA Thesis. Edmonton: University of Alberta, 1987.

Saddlemyer, Ann. "Circus Feminus: 100 Plays by English-Canadian Women." *Room of One's Own*, VIII.2 (July 1983): 78-91.

Saddlemyer, Ann. "Crime in Literature: Canadian Drama." *Rough Justice: Essays on Crime in Literature*, ed. Martin L. Friedland. Toronto: University of Toronto Press, 1991: 214-230.

Saddlemyer, Ann. "Two Canadian Women Playwrights." *Cross-Cultural Studies: American, Canadian and European Literatures 1945-1985*. Ljubljana: Edvard Kardelj University, 1988: 251-256.

Salter, Denis W. "Biocritical Essay. (Im)possible Worlds: The Plays of Sharon Pollock." *First Accession*, eds. Apollonia Steele, and Jean Tener. Calgary: University of Calgary Press, 1989: ix-xxxv.

St. Pierre, Paul Mathew. "Sharon Pollock." *Canadian Writers Since 1960*. 2nd ser. *DLB* 60: 300-306.

Stone-Blackburn, Susan. "Feminism and Metadrama: Role Playing in *Blood Relations*." *Canadian Drama*, 15.2 (1989): 169-178.

Unknown. "Sharon Pollock: *Doc*." *Contemporary Literary Criticism: Yearbook 1987*, 50, ed. Sharon K. Hall. Detroit: Gale Research, 1988: 222-227.

Wallace, Robert, and Cynthia Zimmerman, eds. *The Work: Conversations with English Canadian Playwrights*. Toronto: Coach House Press, 1982: 115-126.

Wylie, Herb. "'Painting the Background': Metadrama and the Fabric of History in Sharon Pollock's *Blood Relations*." *Essays in Theatre*, 15.2 (1996): 191-205.

Zichy, Francis. "Justifying the Ways of Lizzie Borden to Men: The Play Within the Play in *Blood Relations*." *Theatre Annual*, 42 (1987): 61-81.

Zimmerman, Cynthia. "Sharon Pollock: The Making of Warriors." *Playwriting Women: Female Voices in English Canada*. Toronto: Simon & Pierre, 1994: 60-98.

Zimmerman, Cynthia. "Towards a Better, Fairer World: An Interview with Sharon Pollock." *Canadian Theatre Review*, 69 (Winter 1991): 34-38.

Ziraldo, Christiana. *Replaying History: A Study of Sharon Pollock's Walsh, The Komagata Maru Incident, and Blood Relations*, MA Thesis. Guelph: University of Guelph, 1996.

SELECTED REVIEWS

Allen, Bob. "Laughs Aimed at Politicians in a New Play." *Vancouver Province*, 21 March: 35.

Allen, Bob. "Stratford Discovers the West." *Vancouver Province* 5 April 1974: 3.

Anonymous. "Dramatic Feuding: Theatre Calgary's *Walsh* Garners Controversy." *Alberta Report*, 15 (February 15, 1988): 41.

Anonymous. "*The Komagata Maru Incident*: You Can Look For A Message Made Palatable." *Vancouver Sun*, 16 January 1976: 31.

Anonymous. "Playwright Pollock's a Hit in San Diego." *Alberta Report*, 6 (November 23, 1979): 46.

Anonymous. "Sharon Pollock: National Arts Centre." *The Globe and Mail*, 12 May 1983: 25.

Ashley, Audrey M. "Stratford Director, Cast and Playwright's Delight." *Ottawa Citizen*, 25 July 1974: 50.

Baldridge, Harold. "Calgary." *Canadian Theatre Review*, 2 (Spring 1974): 118-120.

Bale, Doug. "Longshot Steals Show at Stratford Festival." *London Free Press*, 25 July 1974.

Brennan, Brian. "*Komagata Maru Incident* Heavily Loaded with Propaganda." *Calgary Herald*, 13 January 1979: A8.

Brennan, Brian. "Playwright's Account of Lizzie Borden Effective Drama." *Calgary Herald*, 14 March 1980: C9.

Brennan, Brian. "Plays Bogs Down in Enigmatic Historical Difficulties." *Calgary Herald*, 12 January 1988: E2.

Brennan, Brian. "Pollock Offers Best Work Yet." *Calgary Herald*, 8 April 1984: F2.

Brennan, Brian. "*Whiskey Six* is Pollock's Best Play Yet." *Calgary Herald*, 11 February 1983: F1.

Brunner, Astrid. "Getting it Straight." *Arts Atlantic*, 9 (Spring-Summer 1989): 59.

Conlogue, Ray. "A Theatrical Gem Reflects the Last, Best West." *The Globe and Mail*, 7 March 1983: 15.

Deakin, Basil. "TAG's *Walsh*: Should Be Stuff of Good Theatre." *Halifax Chronicle Herald*, 14 June 1984: 42.

Dibbelt, Dan. "Walsh." *Windspeaker*, 5 (January 29, 1988): 14.

Doolittle, Joyce. "Walsh." *NeWest Review*, 13 (April 1988): 13.

Downton, Dawn Rae. "Blood Relations." *Arts Atlantic*, 9 (Winter 1989): 62-63.

Fraser, Matthew. "*Doc* May Be Tough Pill for New Brunswick." *The Globe and Mail*, 7 March 1986: A12.

Freeman, Brian. "In Review: *The Komagata Maru Incident*." *Scene Changes*, V.9 (December 1977): 20-21.

Freedman, Adele. "NAC Brings Little to Wild West Yarn." *The Globe and Mail*, 12 May 1983: 25.

Garebian, Keith. "In Review: *One Tiger to a Hill*." *Scene Changes*, VIII.6 (September/October 1980): 37-38.

Godfrey, Stephen. "Debate Soars Above Earthbound Historical Drama." *The Globe and Mail*, 29 January 1988: A18.

Hale, Amanda. "Family Flashback." *Broadside*, 6 (November 1984): 11.

Hustak, Alan. "Sharon Pollock's Triumph: A Hit for Theatre Calgary's New Boss." *Alberta Report*, 11 (April 30, 1984): 54-55.

Johnson, Bryan. "Sikh's Play, *Komagata Maru*, Bitter and Austere, But True." *The Globe and Mail*, 24 October 1977: 15.

Loukes, Randee. "*Whiskey Six*: Observations of a First Performance." *ACTH Newsletter*, 7 (Fall 1983): 17-18.

Milliken, Paul. "In Review: *Generations*." *Scene Changes*, IX.4 (June 1981): 39-40.

Peterson, Maureen. "Centaur's *Blood Relations* Everything A Play Should Be." *Montreal Gazette*, 9 January 1982: 34.

Portman, Jamie. "Calgary I." *Canadian Theatre Review*, 1 (Winter 1974): 118-120.

Portman, Jamie. "Calgary II." *Canadian Theatre Review*, 2 (Spring 1974): 121-123.

Portman, Jamie. "Sharon Pollock Demonstrates Immense Gifts With Latest Play." *Calgary Herald*, 20 March 1980: D1.

Portman, Jamie. "*Walsh* Signals Red-Letter Event for TOL." *Calgary Herald*, 9 November 1973.

Rich, Frank. "Theatre: *Tiger to a Hill* Canadian Prison Drama." *New York Times*, 14 November 1980: C3.

Webster, J. "Another Stage Triumph for Sharon (Pollock)." *Atlantic Advocate*, 64 (August 1974): 50.

Whittaker, Herbert. "Canadian West at Stratford." *The Globe and Mail*, 22 July 1974: 14.

Whittaker, Herbert. "*Walsh* Beautiful, Tedious Too." *The Globe and Mail*, 13 November 1973: 16.

Whittaker, Herbert. "*Walsh* Serves Up Sad History Straight." *The Globe and Mail*, 25 July 1974: 13.

Contributors

Diane Bessai was Professor of English at the University of Alberta, Edmonton. She has published extensively on Canadian drama, particularly in the area of documentary drama and collective creation: *Playwrights of Collective Creation* was published by Simon & Pierre in 1992. For NeWest Press, she has been the series editor for sixteen publications of Canadian plays, including *NeWest Plays by Women, Blood Relations and Other Plays, Showing West: Three Prairie Docu-Dramas*. She is currently researching the history of Edmonton theatre.

Kathy Chung is a Ph.D. candidate at the Graduate Centre for the Study of Drama at the University of Toronto. Her research interests are Canadian theatre and arts history. Her dissertation is on the drama of Sharon Pollock. She was the assistant editor of *Sursum Corda!: The Collected Letters of Malcom Lowry, Vol. Two: 1947-1957*, ed. Sherrill E. Grace, and the illustrator and co-editor, with Sherrill E. Grace of *A Quiet Game and Other Stories*, a volume of juvenilia by Margaret Atwood.

Heidi Holder is Assistant Professor of English at Central Michigan University. She has published essays on British, Irish, and Canadian theatre in *University of Toronto Quarterly, Journal of Modern Literature*, and *Essays in Theatre*, and chapters in *Acts of Supremacy: The British Empire and the Stage, Reassessing the Achievement of J. M. Synge* and *Playwriting and Women in Nineteenth-Century Britain*. She is currently at work on a book about working-class women in Victorian London.

Anne F. Nothof is Professor of English at Athabasca University, Alberta. She has published essays on British and Canadian playwrights, including Hare, Gray, French, Moher, Reaney, Highway, and Pollock, and on prairie and feminist drama. Her essay, "Staging a Woman Painter's Life: Six Versions of Emily Carr," was published in *Mosaic* (September 1998). She has recently edited an anthology of plays for NeWest Press entitled *Ethnicities: Plays from the New West* (1999).

Robert Nunn is a full Professor in the Department of Fine Arts at Brock University, St. Catharine's, Ontario. He has published essays on Canadian playwrights David French and Judith Thompson, and his articles, "Canada Incognita: Has Quebec Theatre Discovered English Canadian Plays (*Theatrum* 1991), and "Flickering lights and declaiming bodies: semiosis in film and theatre" (*TRIC* 1996), received the Association for Canadian Theatre Research's Richard Plant Award. His article on Toronto theatre critic Ray Conlogue appears in *Establishing Our Boundaries: English-Canadian Theatre Criticism*, ed. Anton Wagner, University of Toronto Press, 1999.

Malcolm Page is Professor of English at Simon Fraser University, Vancouver. He has published extensively in contemporary drama, twentieth-century English literature, and Canadian theatre history. For Methuen Drama, he has written *Files* on British playwrights Ayckbourn, Osborne, Pinter, Shaffer, Stoppard, and Arden. He regularly contributes a report on the Vancouver theatre scene to *Plays International*.

Susan Stratton (formerly Susan Stone-Blackburn) is Professor of English at the University of Calgary. Her book, *Robertson Davies, Playwright: A Search for the Self on the Canadian Stage*, was published in 1985. Her articles on Canadian drama have appeared in *Essays in Theatre, Canadian Theatre Review, Canadian Drama,* and *Canadian Literature,* and in the collections, *Woman as Artist, Women and Social Location,* and the *Oxford Companion to Canadian Theatre*.

Craig Walker is Assistant Professor in the Department of Drama at Queen's University, Kingston, Ontario. He has acted with companies at the Stratford and Shaw Festivals, and the National Arts Centre. His book, *Desperate Wilderness: Canadian Dramatic Imagination and Western Tradition*, will be published by McGill-Queen's Press in 1999. He has also published articles in *Modern Drama, Theatre Research in Canada, Australasian Drama Studies, Journal of Dramatic Theory and Criticism, Journal of Canadian Studies,* and *Canadian Theatre Review*. In 1997, Craig was named Artistic Director of Theatre Kingston. His musical, *Chantecler,* was workshopped at the People's Theatre Kingston in 1998.